Conversations About Social Psychology

Conversations About

SOCIAL PSYCHOLOGY

Edited by Howard Burton

Ideas Roadshow conversations present a wealth of candid insights from some of the world's leading experts, generated through a focused yet informal setting. They are explicitly designed to give non-specialists a uniquely accessible window into frontline research and scholarship that wouldn't otherwise be encountered through standard lectures and textbooks.

Over 100 Ideas Roadshow conversations have been held since our debut in 2012, covering a wide array of topics across the arts and sciences.

All Ideas Roadshow conversations are available both as part of a collection or as an individual eBook.

See www.ideasroadshow.com for a full listing of all titles.

Copyright ©2020 Open Agenda Publishing. All rights reserved.

ISBN: 978-1-77170-126-6 (pb)
ISBN: 978-1-77170-125-9 (eBook)

Edited, with preface and all introductions written by Howard Burton.

All *Ideas Roadshow Conversations* use Canadian spelling.

Contents

TEXTUAL NOTE..7

PREFACE 8

BEING SOCIAL
A CONVERSATION WITH ROY BAUMEISTER

    Introduction...19
    I. Psychology, Eventually..23
    II. A Discipline Evolves..30
    III. The Energetic Agent..34
    IV. A Philosophical Digression................................44
    V. Free Will..57
    VI. Cultural Distinctiveness....................................64
    VII. Numbed By Rejection 69
    Continuing the Conversation..................................78

MINDSETS
GROWING YOUR BRAIN
A CONVERSATION WITH CAROL DWECK

    Introduction...81
    I. Fixed Beginnings..87
    II. Confronted by Young Wisdom..........................90
    III. The Genius Defense..95
    IV. Good and Bad Praise...99
    V. Getting Personal..102
    VI. Brainsets..107
    VII. Gender Differences..111
    VIII. Getting the Message Out..............................114
    IX. Practical Tips..117
    X. Diversity and Universality................................121
    XI. New Horizons..125
    XII. The Big Picture...128
    Continuing the Conversation................................130

THE MIND-BODY PROBLEM
A CONVERSATION WITH JANKO TIPSAREVIC

Introduction 133
I. On Nietzsche and Tennis 139
II. Lost Opportunities 143
III. Commitment 147
IV. Breaking Through 151
V. Tennis as a Team Sport 160
VI. Achieving Potential 165
VIII. Winner Take All? 170

THE SCIENCE OF EMOTIONS
A CONVERSATION WITH BARBARA FREDRICKSON

Introduction 177
I. Psychological Beginnings 182
II. Emotions, Scientifically 186
III. Positive vs. Negative Emotions 190
IV. Positive Psychology Emerges 194
V. Broaden and Build 196
VI. Emotional Measurement 198
VII. The Undoing Effect 203
VIII. Taking Charge 206
IX. Responses 211
X. Personal Flourishing 216
XI. Leveraging Positivity 219
Continuing the Conversation 222

CRITICAL SITUATIONS
A CONVERSATION WITH PHILIP ZIMBARDO

Introduction 225
I. Origins 231
II. A Formative Quarantine 237
III. Increasing Awareness 243
IV. Situation Stanford 252
V. The Aftermath 266
VI. Outright Denial 273
VII. Learning Our Lessons? 280
VIII. The Flip Side 286
IX. Spreading The Word 294
X. A New Gender Gap 300
Continuing the Conversation 303

Textual Note

The contents of this book are based upon separate filmed conversations with Howard Burton and each of the five featured experts.

Roy Baumeister is Professor of Psychology at the University of Queensland. This conversation occurred on October 31, 2014.

Carol S. Dweck is the Lewis and Virginia Eaton Professor of Psychology at Stanford University. This conversation occurred on March 19, 2014.

Janko Tipsarevic is the founder and CEO of Tipsarevic Tennis Academy in Belgrade, Serbia. He is a former professional tennis player, with a career-high singles ranking of world No. 8. This conversation occurred on August 23, 2013.

Barbara Fredrickson is Kenan Distinguished Professor of Psychology at the University of North Carolina at Chapel Hill. This conversation occurred on October 29, 2014.

Philip Zimbardo is Professor Emeritus of Psychology at Stanford University. This conversation occurred on September 29, 2014.

Howard Burton is the creator and host of Ideas Roadshow and was Founding Executive Director of Perimeter Institute for Theoretical Physics.

Preface

"Social psychology" is one of those curious expressions that makes perfect sense until you start reflecting more deeply upon it, at which point you invariably develop the uncomfortable sensation that not only is the term itself much more slippery than you had thought, but the surrounding concepts designed to frame it begin to appear almost equally fuzzy.

One often-invoked reference point comes from a 1989 paper, "Attitudes: Evaluating the social world" by Baron, Byrne and Suls, where social psychology is defined as, *"The scientific field that seeks to understand the nature and causes of individual behavior in social situations"*; while others say things like, *"The study of the manner in which the personality, attitudes, motivations, and behavior of the individual influence and are influenced by social groups".*

It all seems straightforward enough: Social psychology is that part of psychology that focuses on how our social milieu impinges on our thoughts and actions—which, in turn, has a corresponding impact on that surrounding milieu itself.

But then, reflection sets in: *But we **all** live in groups. Aside from a few hermits—all of whom can be safely placed in the "abnormal psychology" box for the time being at least—**everyone** has a "surrounding milieu" that significantly influences individual thoughts, feelings and consequent action. To what extent, then, is it even possible to talk about a meaningful theory of psychology that **isn't** social psychology?*

Well, it's a matter of degree, of course. But on the whole, it seems to me that the closer psychology veers towards neuroscience, and the more the focus is on interpreting findings in terms of brain networks and biological structures, the less significant these social factors become.

If I'm trying to understand how auditory illusions work or assess how bilingualism impacts my executive control network, it's likely that most associated social factors can be disregarded, at least in the early stages of our inquiries. It's not that these factors are *irrelevant*—I might hear different things depending on what others expect me to hear, or think somewhat differently in another language due to corresponding cultural factors—but in none of those cases do social influences strike me as necessary to take into account in order to develop a general comprehensive understanding of the phenomenon in question.

And what seems to make "social psychology" different is precisely that: now social factors *are* fundamental to our understanding. So perhaps a more reasonable way to begin our inquiries is not so much by rigorously defining what social psychology *is*, but objectively assessing which aspects of psychological understanding inherently depend on social factors.

But there's the rub. Because it turns out that, for a combination of factors—political, cultural, philosophical and more—evaluating the impact other people have on our behaviour has consistently been minimized—if not deliberately overlooked—both in professional psychology and society at large.

As **Philip Zimbardo** emphatically puts it:

> *"We all want to believe that we are the masters of our fate, that our behaviour comes from inner free will, from inner determination. We all want to deny that anything we do is influenced by other people or situational forces. My mission in life has been to present the case for situational power and situational awareness. When I wrote The Lucifer Effect, I added the idea that systems are the power behind creating, maintaining, and potentially changing those situations.*

"But people don't want to buy that. All attempts at "changing", "improving," or "modifying" human behaviour are focused solely on the individual level. Therapy, incarceration, sterilization, nutrition, exercise—those things only focus on the individual level. There's almost no program for changing situations, because it's considered too complicated. Even though we can demonstrate that, for example, PTSD therapy for returning veterans has no effect, we just keep doing it. We know that prisoners get little or no rehabilitation and, in less than three years, 70% are back in prison. Why? Because you put them back in the same situation they were in before. The situation is corrupt, so they end up back in prison."

In fact, as ironic as it is, this tendency to focus on isolated individuals even pervades the domain of social psychology itself, as **Roy Baumeister** vividly recalls:

"When I was in graduate school, I was reading a lot and trying to absorb the information from the psychological literature. There was a tendency to explain everything as basic processes happening inside the person; and I thought, Well, maybe there's more of an interpersonal dimension going on that people only really give lip service to—after all, it is social psychology. There were a lot of discussions of people being concerned about their self-esteem and how they'll react to failure or criticism or success as it depended on their sense of self-esteem. And I remember thinking—and this ended up being my dissertation—Well, maybe people are a little concerned with that but they're probably a lot more concerned with how other people esteem them.

"So we gave people praise or criticism either confidentially or publicly. The effect on the self-esteem should be the same—what it tells you about yourself is identical—but boy, they reacted much more if somebody else knew about it. So I've been a bit of a contrarian in social psychology saying, "We need to be more social: people relate to others; a lot of things are much more interpersonal than we've assumed". There was this general sense that, Well, OK, people interact, but what they do and say to each other is a product of other things going on inside them.

> *"And I tried to turn that around and say, "Inner processes serve interpersonal functions: what's going on inside you is there to facilitate relating to others". Basically, nature doesn't care what's going on inside you and what your self-esteem is or how happy you are or anything like that—it doesn't have any clear effect on your survival or reproduction. But what other people think of you turns out to be absolutely crucial. For a species like ours, if others don't accept you, you're not going to survive, let alone reproduce."*

Roy's specific invocation of evolutionary biology is particularly worth highlighting, as often "social psychology" is viewed as a sort of "watered-down, touchy-feely" sort of discipline with its unrigorous notions like "peer pressure" and "group dynamics". But what is typically unappreciated is that invoking such "merely descriptive" terminology is nothing less than an inevitable consequence of trying to understand a deeply complex phenomenon for which no suitable framework exists and hardly betokens a desire to act "unscientifically".

And so we find **Barbara Fredrickson**, just like Roy Baumeister, approaching her psychological investigations of positive emotions with evolutionary considerations first and foremost in her mind.

> *"We had these templates for understanding the evolutionary value of emotions. As the science of emotions began to develop, there was kind of a "cookie cutter" template used for all emotions, which was: emotions promote specific action tendencies, which had helped our ancestors survive threats to life and limb. And if you use that for understanding the evolutionary value of emotions, it's easy to just leave the positive emotions out. There were theories of emotion that were saying, "This is how emotions evolved", that didn't even mention positive emotions, which I find pretty amusing, given their obvious existence.*

> *"What I did in my early work is to point out that we can't use the same theoretical framework to understand the value of positive emotions. In particular, the timescale is different. Whereas the adaptive value of a negative emotion is during the moment of threat—preparing you*

> to do some action that is evolutionarily advantageous—with positive emotions there's no clear action tendency that's going to save your skin right at that moment, because, most often, there is no threat. -I argued that they have a clear psychology: they broaden people's mindsets. And that's beneficial, not in that particular moment, but in the longer term. If you've had more of those moments—those 'broadened awareness' moments—you've accrued more resources that end up filling out your survival toolkit."

Similar to Roy Baumeister's argument, this "survival toolkit" Fredrickson mentions is *inherently* social—our ability to survive is not just as individuals, but as active members of a group, with all of the accompanying dynamics that this entails.

But while evolutionary arguments are ultimately necessary for understanding how we came to be the way we are, some social psychologists naturally focus on how our present state might be significantly improved, investigating to what extent a deeper understanding of social factors might enable us to flourish.

Enter **Carol Dweck**, pioneer of the landmark distinction between a growth mindset and fixed mindset.

> "In my work, a mindset is a belief people have about whether their basic qualities are just fixed, given, inborn, or represent something that can change and develop. For example, some people have a fixed mindset about their intellectual abilities. They think their intelligence is just fixed: you have a certain amount and that's that. What we find is that when people have this view, they don't want to do hard things that might reveal some sense of inadequacy, and they don't stick to hard things because they feel dumb.
>
> "But other people have a growth mindset. They believe their basic abilities can be developed through hard work, good strategies, and help and mentoring from others. They don't think everyone's the same, or that anyone can be Einstein, but they understand that people don't become the people that they become without effort—just as Einstein didn't become Einstein until he worked at it. So people with a growth

mindset are more likely to take on hard challenges and stick to them, because that's how you learn and grow."

Once again, we're presented with a clear and compelling framework of how the real or imagined views of others—being perceived as inadequate, not measuring up to established ideals, being judged by one's peers or the wider society—can have a strong and lasting effect on personal behaviour—indeed, not just for one specific action we might be engaged in, but for virtually every one of them.

All four of these academics—Philip Zimbardo, Roy Baumeister, Barbara Fredrickson and Carol Dweck—are renowned social psychologists who have built highly successful careers out of illustrating the vital importance of appropriately considering social factors on our beliefs, desires and consequent actions.

The fifth person in this collection, on the other hand, is neither a psychologist nor an academic at all, but rather a former top 10 professional tennis player. What, you might ask, is going on *there*? Why is **Janko Tipsarevic** included in a collection about ***social psychology***? Why not **Lisa Feldman Barrett**, say, who has also done pioneering research on the science of emotions, or **Elizabeth Loftus**, who has tangibly demonstrated the strong impact of social and situational factors on our memories?

Well, there are actually several reasons, but the principal point is to tangibly demonstrate how various aspects of these core ideas play out in the world around us.

Here, for example, is Tipsarevic reflecting on the enormous impact the particularly social atmosphere of Davis Cup has on his thoughts and actions:

> *"The Davis Cup is my favourite competition in the whole year. I have a feeling that I was born to play a team sport, because I really feel like a team player. There are a couple of guys on tour who've played more matches than me and more years consecutively—maybe Lleyton Hewitt—but not too many, I promise you. The main reason why I play*

> is because I like my teammates so much. If this week were a struggle for me, if I was thinking: Oh my God, I have to spend a week with these guys I don't like or whatever, I would never have had the kind of run that I've had.

> "This is so much fun. I have so much energy during the event, I feel like a teenager. The three of us have dinner and then go into a room and just talk about anything. It's something that you don't have on tour. Generally, you finish your match, finish your practice, you stretch with your physiotherapist and you go to your room to watch a movie and recover and that's it. These Davis Cup weeks are really, really special."

And here is Tipsarevic talking about his philosophy of how a coach can influence a top player's performance:

> "A good coach, in my experience, will tell you stuff when you need to hear it. It's not about pointing out mistakes—that doesn't really help. It really depends on the situation. I believe in simplicity in terms of coaching because if you feed your player too much information then he starts over-thinking and not focusing on the right things. A coach should point out one, two or three things max that should be focused on and just let the player find his own way. Because, as I said, at the end of the day you are completely alone on the court. The coach's job is just to push you in the right direction so you find the highway."

And here again is Tipsarevic talking—in his own words, of course—about the power of adopting a growth mindset.

> "I am much, much better in the last two or three years and this is one of the reasons why I broke into the top 10. Before, I was finding all sorts of stupid things and maybe even excuses to get upset about, to spend energy on; and then when the tennis match came I knew that I hadn't given 100%, which meant that, psychologically, I was less disappointed if I lost. I'd say to myself, Sure, if I would do these things differently I could play better but who cares? It's like an alibi that you have in your mind which makes you deal a little bit better with a loss.

"After we won the Davis Cup I felt so much joy and so much happiness. And I remember thinking to myself, at the age of 25 or 26, Time is flying: I'm not a kid anymore. And I thought to myself, I really want to make the most of my career. Because I knew that when I stopped playing tennis and hung my racket on the wall and said I'm done, I would have this huge regret that I would need to live with for the rest of my life if I didn't really do my best. It's OK to fail. But it's not OK not to try."

Slotting the candid admissions of a world-class tennis player into a "psychology collection" as the designated "sports psychology" component likely wouldn't raise an eyebrow, while explicitly incorporating his ruminations in a "social psychology collection" will probably seem very odd to many.

And that's a large part of the problem.

Being Social

A conversation with Roy Baumeister

Introduction

The Human Animal

Roy Baumeister is one of the most cited social psychologists around. Which is why when he refers to himself as something of an outsider, it's a bit hard to take it seriously. But that doesn't mean it isn't true.

As it happens, Roy's sense of disconnect with the prevailing winds of social psychology began very early on in his career, when he was starting his doctorate.

> "When I was in graduate school, I was reading a lot and trying to absorb the information from the psychological literature. There was a tendency to explain everything as basic processes happening inside the person; and I thought, Well, maybe there's more of an interpersonal dimension going on that people are only really give lip service to—after all, it is **social** psychology.
>
> "There were a lot of discussions of people being concerned about their self-esteem and how they'll react to failure or criticism or success as it depended on their sense of self-esteem.
>
> "And I remember thinking—and this ended up being my dissertation—Well, maybe people are a little concerned with that but they're probably a lot more concerned with how **other** people esteem them."

That dissertation work turned out to be *The Need To Belong*, his highly influential work with Mark Leary that tangibly demonstrated how our human urge to connect with others had a real, measurable impact on a wide range of measurable aspects of our mental and physical well-being.

Strangely enough, however, despite its success, *The Need To Belong* hardly changed social psychology in the way that Roy had initially hoped, as by and large the general domain of psychology has had a very difficult time breaking free from its preconceived notions of interpreting human dynamics from an individualistic perspective.

> *"I've been a bit of a contrarian in social psychology, saying '**We need to be more social**'. And indeed, after **The Need To Belong**, social psychology went a lot more **inside** the single mind. Most of social psychology is now done by having someone sit behind a computer and make ratings, which is a very solitary activity."*

That is clearly ironic, but it is much more besides: a strong refusal to embrace our basic human biology and see the larger picture of the human condition in terms of our driving evolutionary history.

> *"I've been on this campaign to say, '**You know, people relate to others; a lot of things are much more interpersonal than we've assumed**'. There was this general sense that, Well, OK, people interact, but what they do and say to each other is a product of other things going on inside them.*
>
> *"And I tried to turn that around and say, '**Inner processes serve interpersonal functions: what's going on inside you is there to facilitate relating to others**'.*
>
> *"Basically, nature doesn't care what's going on inside you and what your self-esteem is or how happy you are or anything like that—it doesn't have any clear effect on your survival or reproduction.*
>
> *"But what other people think of you turns out to be absolutely crucial. For a species like ours, if others don't accept you, you're not going to survive, let alone reproduce."*

Seamlessly combining biological and psychological thinking is a hallmark of Roy's approach throughout his entire career, from recognizing essential energetic factors involved with willpower and decision-making, to framing free will in evolutionary biological terms, to measuring the numbness associated with social rejection as a form of analgesic response.

Doing so isn't just some form of trendy "interdisciplinarity"—it is nothing less than a way of thinking deeper, placing the human condition in its broadest possible context so as to develop a deeper understanding not just of how individuals make decisions, but how human societies and cultures arise and flourish. Because—and here's this central point again that strangely needs to be emphasized—human beings *don't* actually live independently from each other. We live in groups.

> *"Like all other animals, we have to solve the problems of survival and reproduction. You need a biological strategy—every living thing has some strategy for doing that—but ours is a very unusual one as human beings: we create these complex social systems with meaning, with shared information, with interlocking roles and identities and moral obligations and so forth, all of which works very well for us. As a result, we live a lot better than most other creatures, but it needs a lot more psychological capabilities to successfully function in a culture.*
>
> *"So the traits that define us as human—and that's not all the traits, we share many with other animals—the ones that set us apart are evolutionary adaptations to make possible this new strategy of living in a civilized culture."*

Civilization, then, is the natural culmination of psychology and biology.

Well, what else could it possibly be?

The Conversation

I. Psychology, Eventually
Third time lucky

HB: I'd like to start by talking a little bit about your background. I understand that you played the guitar. Did you play it for a long time? Was music a big thing in your life?

RB: Yes, my mother's side was musical—she played the trumpet and she was in some of those little Dixieland bands when she was young. I took trumpet lessons for a while, but when I got braces, it was really hard to sustain, so I stopped.

Then, when I left for college she said, *"Why don't you just play the guitar? You don't want to waste your musical talent. If you have a guitar you can just lean it up against the wall and grab it every now and then"*—her point being that trumpet was an instrument you have to play every day in order to keep your mouth muscles strong.

HB: Well, you knew how to read music, obviously; but you had never taken any guitar lessons, up to that point?

RB: No, I had never had any guitar lessons or even really understood the chords and things all that well. But I got a book and taught myself and I practiced pretty assiduously every day for ten years—I got to be in some bands, nothing very good but it was fun. Once I became a professor, I had to put it aside for a while but a while ago I took it up again. I'm getting old now—the thumbs are starting to get arthritis—and I just wondered, *"Are there no old guitarists?"*

HB: Well, there's B.B. King.

RB: Yes, he's one. He's ancient now—he was old when I was learning in the '70s—he must be over 100 or something now. Anyway, I noticed that in a lot of bands they have old piano and trumpet players but no old guitarists, so I think it's that the arthritis gradually undermines your ability and you start to cheat on a solo because you think to yourself, *Well, it's going to hurt to play that one.* I should switch to play the piano or something.

HB: You would think that it would affect pianists as well but there are many precedents of older pianists who play awfully well—perhaps not quite as well as they did in their prime, but still.

RB: I find piano is not nearly as hard on you; guitar you really have to press and hold and there's no real substitute, whereas piano is a little easier—it was just my thumbs that started to hurt, so it's really a small issue if I really hit the keys hard, but a lot of the other fingers are doing the work, whereas for the guitar the thumb really has to hold it all together and hold the pick.

HB: Moving laterally a little bit now to your interest in psychology. Was this something that you'd been gravitating towards in high school—or even earlier perhaps—or not at all?

RB: Not at all. In high school I was good at math. I wanted to go and be a mathematician and even went to college based on who had the best math department.

HB: You went to Princeton for your undergraduate, right? You went there to study math?

RB: Yes, that's correct. I guess there are a lot of kids who come there with that idea and then they see higher math and get put into really advanced stuff that's very detached from anything you could relate to. I did alright in it but all the other courses were so much more interesting.

Those were also the hippie days and I thought you had to be relevant and all that, so I went on to study philosophy and religion and tackle the big questions like, *Is religion just a product of human psychology or mental states? Philosophically, what do we know? What's right and wrong?*—all those big questions.

I did that for a bit but then my parents kind of baulked and said, "*You can't get a job in philosophy, it doesn't really pay*"—it was just at the time when people were starting to consider that as a criterion for college, it was the transition between the '60s to the '70s and the economy was tightening up. So they said to me, "*If you want to go to law school or something, then you could be a philosophy major*". So I interviewed some lawyers and got a sense of what their life was like and decided almost immediately that I didn't want to do that.

HB: Just to back up a bit—you're in second year now?

RB: Yes, after second year I needed to declare a major.

HB: And you actually went and interviewed some lawyers? That's pretty forward thinking.

RB: Well, I just wanted to know what that life was like. Every guy I talked to really liked being a lawyer, but it didn't sound like anything I wanted to do. At that time, I had been over in Germany in foreign study doing philosophy and I had read some of Freud's books. The philosophers were debating right and wrong based on analyzing the concepts, while Freud said, "*Well, let's look at how people actually, historically, come up with right and wrong and how children learn it and how societies develop these ideas.*"

I thought it was very interesting how you could use an empirical approach to address these things, so I suggested that to my parents as a possible compromise.

I remember my father's reaction when I said, "*How about if I major in psychology?*" he just responded, "*You'd be wasting your brain!*"

He didn't think it was a field for smart people, which he hoped I would be. To his credit, however, he went and looked it up and, as it happened, he was working for Standard Oil Company and there were some psychologists on the payroll who were earning more than he was.

So he came home and said, *"Well, I guess you can make a living doing that so, OK, if that's what you want to do, go do it"*—so psychology it was.

HB: Did you ever convince him that it wasn't wasting one's brain, by the way, independent of being able to earn a living? Those are two different issues, after all.

RB: Well, he's 87 now, and we just moved him into an assisted living home and we had to get rid of most of his stuff, but I noticed that he brought along copies of a few of my books. So, he has them—whether he's read them or not, I can't say.

HB: That could be paternal pride, though—it might not have anything to do with his respect for psychology as a discipline.

RB: Well, it's probably getting late to find out, but he hasn't said too many negative things about psychology. I think, to him, a lot turned on the money issue and the fact that you could make a living at it and do well—that's what distinguished it from philosophy in his mind, so it seemed okay.

HB: OK, back to your story: you were given the green light to continue, you're entering your junior year at Princeton as a psychology major—how did it go from there? What sort of courses were you taking? How did your interests develop? You mentioned Freud just now, were you thinking more about empirical studies right away in terms of human motivations? Were you looking at abnormal psychology? What was your area of interest at the time?

RB: Back then, I was just a kid and didn't know that much. I thought, *Well, maybe I should just be like Freud. I could become a therapist and make money and cure the sick*, but—like Freud, himself actually—I was less interested in helping people than in finding out the truth about human nature and the ultimate questions.

So then I thought that I could write books based on the clinical observations but that was no longer viable, that bridge had been burned: you can't study the mentally ill and write about human nature on that basis. And Freudian psychoanalysis was just starting to decline in influence and popularity at that time as well.

HB: Did you study that formally at Princeton?

RB: Well, the first class that I had was by somebody who admired Freud, so we spent a good part of the semester on Freud, but I learned a lot of other things too. It was also a time when enrolments in psychology had gone up enormously, so everything was over-burdened. Departments that were designed to have 20 students a year suddenly had 100. That was the case at Princeton, too—within two or three years, it had gone from a stable 20 a year to 100 or so per class.

HB: Why was that, do you think?

RB: It had to do with changes in fashion, changes in the zeitgeist—interest in social science was stimulated by the '60s activism and the hippies and all of that.

The hippies kind of had two phases; one was the political phase and one was the more mystical, self-exploration phase. There was a brief surge in sociology enrolments just before psychology—they went up very precipitously and then went right back down—it somehow didn't catch on—but there was a brief time when lots of people did sociology. The psychology one then turned out to be more durable. I was a good little boy from Cleveland and didn't have much background with hippies or anything and was exposed to all these wild ideas.

HB: Did you have short hair, by the way, when you went to Princeton?

RB: Oh yes. It might have just been a little bit longer than it is now because I'd been in a Motown band in high school that I played trumpet for until the braces got bad. At any rate, it was still fairly short when I got to Princeton.

HB: Okay, so you did that and then you decided that you were interested in doing graduate work. How did that work, exactly?

RB: Well, I always thought I would get a PhD. I wanted to be a professor as soon as I stopped wanting to be a general in the Civil War at the end of elementary school. Partly, my father had looked around and he had an uncle who was a professor and he thought that was a pretty good life. I remember, one year, we had to do reports on careers and I chose the professor to do mine, looked it up and it seemed like a pretty good deal. I remember that you could make as much as $30,000 as a full-time professor, which was a lot more money than it is now.

HB: And it was certainly easier than being a general in the Civil War, given the time period.

RB: Yes, the prospects were better. So that was always on my mind. At first it was going to math, then philosophy and, finally, psychology. The clinical psychology professors seemed to have a pretty good situation because they could do clinical work and make extra money, talk to people and so on.

But it was very difficult to get into clinical psychology—they were getting hundreds of applications for every place. Even coming from a good school with good grades, it was almost just a lottery there.

And I was also realizing that doing therapy was not as appealing as it sounded from reading Freud's book. Some people described it as spending an hour a day, every day, for several years with some very unpleasant people listening to them complaining about their problems—that was psychoanalysis. It didn't seem that that suited me terribly well either.

I could also see that psychoanalysis was in decline and it wasn't clear where the field was going. It turned out to be a lucky thing for me, because I thought to myself, *Well, I'll just go into social psychology.* I had had a couple of great professors who were interested in that, and so while I thought I likely wouldn't make as much money doing that, it would likely turn out to be a decent, satisfying career.

Whereas it was clear to me that, to be a clinician, if you could just get into graduate school you'd be set for life, but there were real difficulties both getting in and the lifestyle afterwards.

And it turns out that there were other difficulties there too. Several clinicians I know have dropped out by now because the field's gone through such terrible changes and it's become difficult to make a living. Some said their salary hadn't really gone up in 20 years because the insurance payments have drastically increased. So the old idea of psychoanalysis where somebody pays you a large amount of money for every hour and that you have that income, steadily, for years, is just no longer the case.

Questions for Discussion:

1. Why do you think that the burst of interest in sociology in the early 1970s was so short-lived compared to that of psychology?

2. Do you think that, on the whole, Freud's influence on psychology has been positive or negative?

3. To what extent can one characterize the temperament required to be a successful clinical psychologist? Do universities do a good enough job at helping students understand whether such a career is for them?

II. A Discipline Evolves
The changing fashions of social psychology

HB: What were the prevailing issues of the day in social psychology when you began graduate school?

RB: They were disappointing to me coming from philosophy: the issues being debated struck me as very "un-profound".

There was Cognitive Dissonance Theory: the idea that people try to be consistent—you don't want to say one thing and do something else—so if people do something else, then they'll change what they say to rationalize it. I've come to appreciate it over the years but, initially, it seemed fairly obvious—just a form of consistency.

Another idea prevalent at the time was Attribution Theory, where people draw inferences about what's happening in the world like, *What kind of person is this that I'm talking to?* or *Why did that person do that?* or *Why did I get a bad grade on this test?* and so on. Basically, instead of sophisticated analyses of what was going on, they simplified it down to, *Was it internal to the person or external to the situation?* and other very simple frameworks like that.

So I had a little bit of a struggle there to reconcile myself to working in a field that struck me intellectually quite primitive, but that turned out to be lucky too. The field of social psychology became much more intellectually diverse and open—perhaps still not as sharp as philosophy, but they don't do anything but think up theories—and it's a much more intellectually lively, stimulating and challenging discipline now than it was in the 1970s.

HB: Of course, as a social psychologist, you have recourse to this vast spectrum of empirical devices and avenues: you can go out and test people on this reaction or that reaction and you can develop an incredible amount of data—so you have this tapestry that you can weave of going back and forth between intellectual hypothesis and verification.

There is, of course, a great deal of skill in being able to choose the right question, conduct the experiment in a very particular way and so on—there is a whole wealth of options which is now open to you if you're interested in exploring human behaviour and human motivations that you simply don't have as a philosopher.

RB: Yes, one of my professors in graduate school had that same view. He said, "*What attracted me to psychology was an experimental approach to philosophy: you can do studies to actually resolve questions and reach some answers.*"

It changes our focus. In philosophy, if you're interested in right and wrong or responsibility or knowledge or whatever, they'll debate the borderline cases at great length, but in psychology we can focus on the prototype and not worry about the borderlines.

One of my ambitions is to write a social science book on each of the big questions of philosophy. I wrote a book on evil, for example (*Evil: Inside Human Violence and Cruelty*). As a philosopher you debate things like, What is evil? and Where do you draw the line?

But I didn't need to do that: I could just take a broad, loose definition and use our data to develop the causal processes, to measure things, to show what makes people do things and how they experience things.

They're both valuable fields. I'm not saying one is better than the other, but right now it's a good time to be in psychology because there are still lots of interesting questions.

But in philosophy, physics, chemistry—those other fields that have been around for a long time—you have to go a long way to get to the front lines, and a lot of things have been discussed, worked on and thought of; whereas there's still a lot that's wide open in psychology.

HB: Right, so there's both the experimental aspect, as well as the intellectual constructs. But then, particularly these days, there's also the biological side of things—it seems like there's almost this three-cornered hat.

So we can begin with addressing core questions and trying to build up some sort of intellectual framework: *What is motivating people? How do people make decisions? How do they stop making decisions? What's actually going on in their thought processes? How do they restrain themselves from succumbing to temptation?* and all that.

Then one can go to a laboratory on the street and start investigating, in a fairly rigorous way, how exactly to develop data that might eventually support one hypothesis versus another.

But equally, one can then turn to physiology—be it neurophysiology or more general biological arguments—and start looking at physical mechanisms in the body that might account for this or that particular action.

It seems to me that you're interested in crossing all of those boundaries and linking all three together. Is that a fair statement?

RB: Yes, to get a full understanding, you have to tie all of that together. There's been a big influx of biological thinking into psychology that was not there when I was in college.

I remember in the personality class that I took, the professor started by saying, *"Well, personality is something that you learn, that you acquire. I don't really think the idea that you're born with some traits is true and if there is any aspect of it, it's not anything that we're interested in".*

That was the zeitgeist, he was not being unusual then but today, no one would say that as a lot of traits seem to be linked to innate predispositions.

Things are very different today, between interest in the physiology of the brain, twin studies on genetic heritability of traits and patterns, examinations of the specific influence of hormones and so on—I think nowadays the problem is that we tend to think a biological understanding will explain too much: there are a lot of people who think that, once we figure out how the brain works, we'll really understand the true causes of everything.

But the brain is just sort of like a switchboard that passes on information, it's not really a cause—we need to look out in the social world to see what's happening there. The brain can't do too much that differs from that—it's best if it figures out what's really going on out there.

So, the causes don't lie in the brain—the brain is just passing along information and working with it. The brain is not why behaviour happens.

Questions for Discussion:

1. To what extent do you think a biological and physiological understanding is necessary for psychological understanding?

2. Do you agree with Roy's view that "causes don't lie in the brain"? How common do you think this view is within cognitive science? For alternative perspectives see, for example, Chapter 3 of **Constructing Our World: The Brain's-Eye View** with Lisa Feldman Barrett and Chapters 5–6 of **Minds and Machines** with Miguel Nicolelis.

III. The Energetic Agent
Yet another reason to eat more ice cream

HB: Since you mentioned causes and the brain, that seems a good opportunity to turn to questions about free will. Many people invoke this notion of "the brain" as if it is something completely independent from "us", and I think it's important to clarify what, in fact, we're actually talking about when we're making these distinctions between "my conscious self" and "my brain" in order to get a clear sense of where, exactly, the line is between the two.

But before we get there, I'd like to talk a little bit about willpower and how your ideas on that combine your experimental results with some biological aspects—my understanding is glucose plays some interesting role in some of these processes—and a general statement of what's actually happening when we are exhibiting or not exhibiting willpower. Tell me about how you became interested in that and what you discovered there.

RB: Well, I'd been studying issues of self and identity for much of my career. I had looked at self-esteem and self-concept and self-awareness and so forth, and self-control or self-regulation was a late one that emerged.

It had been routine when people had conferences on *the self* to say, "*Well, we understand a lot about how people think of themselves and communicate to others and so on, but we don't understand "the self" as an **agent**—how does that work?*" That was the gap; and I wanted to see if I could figure out anything there.

Self-regulation is part of being an agent—it's exerting control over yourself—and the answer that I came to, after a couple years of reading a lot of literature, was that there's some kind of energy involved. Psychology had just not used energy models for so long: we named one of the effects "Ego Depletion" using the Freudian term because he was really the *last* person to say that the self was made partly of energy.

I used to joke when I gave talks that energy models are so far out of fashion that we're not even against them anymore; but it really *did* seem to fit: that willpower or self-control worked like there was some energy that got used up.

I wrote this in a book with two colleagues while I was away on sabbatical and sent it back to my graduate students to read, because I wanted to keep them involved, and one said, "*Well, we can do experiments on this.*"

So we tried a couple of experiments where you'd have people first do one self-control task and then go and do a different self-control task.

HB: What were these self-control tasks exactly?

RB: Well, in the first study, one measure was how long they could squeeze a hand grip—one of those little exercise things—and even after thirty seconds or so it gets harder to do because the spring is working against your hand so you want to release it, which means that it takes self-control to make yourself continue to squeeze.

We had people first watch a movie that was kind of upsetting—wildlife dying and things like that—and we told them to either control their feelings and stifle them down, amplify their feelings and react as strongly as possible, or just let their feelings go—in other words, not exert self-control.

And we showed that changing their emotions in either direction—increasing or decreasing them—seemed to reduce how well they did on the hand-grip test afterwards because they used up some kind of energy trying to control their emotions that they then didn't have for the second task.

My friend Dan Wegner had been reading an article about Tolstoy describing how Tolstoy used to make a bet with his younger brother that he couldn't go five minutes without thinking about a white bear.

The brother would say, "*I do that all the time, I'll take the bet,*" but as soon as he did, he couldn't do it.

So we tried that: we told people to think about anything they wanted but just not a white bear, and we measured how long they kept trying before they gave up on this very difficult puzzle, which was actually unsolvable unbeknownst to them.

HB: You're mean people, you psychologists.

RB: Well, it was hardly traumatic for them. Anyway, sure enough, the people who had tried to shut that thought out of their mind had less willpower, less energy, of some sort, because they gave up much faster on the difficult puzzles we gave them afterwards compared to others—we had a couple of different control groups.

Probably the most famous study from the early one was *The Radish Study*. Dianne Tice, my wife, and I were sitting around in a lab meeting thinking of ways to test this and she said, "*We should get a big bowl of radishes and a big bowl of chocolates and say* **'We really need you in the radish condition,'** *so they have to sit there eating radishes while wishing they had chocolates.*"

So we set up an experiment like that where some were told to eat the chocolates and cookies, others had a no-food control, but the crucial ones were the ones who had to sit there and eat the radishes.

They didn't watch the other people but they were alone in the room with them and we baked the cookies right in the room so it smelled so very delicious and it was awfully tempting.

That was probably the meanest thing we did, but I should say that we let them have a cookie when the study was all over.

HB: **One** cookie? After all that you only gave them one?

RB: Oh, I don't remember.

HB: They probably couldn't eat any more because they were filled with radishes.

RB: They didn't eat that many radishes either, actually.

But the point was that later, in another room, they also gave up faster on another difficult perseverance task.

Anyway, there were about half a dozen kinds of procedures that we used, but you get the idea: you use up your willpower in one thing and then you don't have as much for the next.

HB: So what are the implications of all of this? You look at the question of willpower from an energy perspective—which nobody had done before—and you think to yourself, "*Okay, we developed a hypothesis, we've tested it, and there seems to be some evidence favouring it*". Having done all that, and reached a conclusion, what does this mean? What can I do with this information?

RB: Well, as far as the implications for everyday life, you realize that your self-control, your willpower is not a fixed trait of your character but a fluctuating resource.

Sure some people have more than others to start with, but regardless of that you have more at some times than other times, so it's important to appreciate the demands that are being made on it: the same person in the same situation will make different decisions—including some she might be sorry about later—depending on how much willpower she had at the time: how it's fluctuated and other things she did that same day.

Remember, the idea was to better understand the "agent aspect of the self"—the executive function—so controlling yourself was part of that and making decisions in the world was another.

So we did some experiments to see if, indeed, making a bunch of decisions would then impair your self-control on another task. I remember this study I was particularly interested in—I kind of held my breath on that one more than anything since I'd gotten tenure—thinking to myself, *This could be really big*.

And sure enough it was. It took a while because the decision-making people—the reviewers at the journals—are very picky, but eventually, we got enough data to persuade everybody and published something that effectively said, "*Yes, making choices depletes that same resource.*"

Some people realize intuitively that your willpower gets worn down, but they don't have any sense that making decisions will deplete you in that way. An article in the *New York Times* called *Do You Suffer From Decision Fatigue?* was the most emailed article for weeks on end, and possibly of the entire year, because a lot of people could relate to that.

A year or two after that, we saw an interview that President Obama just decided that he was going to wear the same coloured suits everyday to avoid that energy depletion on a daily basis. He did the same thing with food that he ate, because he has so many other enormous decisions to make.

The decisions that come to him aren't any of the easy ones—the easier ones are made lower down on the chain—so he doesn't want to waste any time or energy on those really tough ones through deciding what to wear or eat.

HB: You can imagine having your national security put at risk by Giorgio Armani—you wouldn't want that situation to actually occur.

So let me ask a follow-up question: I understand this idea about prioritizing energy, and the clear implication seems to be that if you have more energy, you will not only have an easier time making decisions, but you will be able to make *better* decisions.

So that's what I would imagine would happen, but still it's a supposition. Do you have any evidence that having more energy not only makes it easier for us to make decisions, but increases the likelihood that we'll make *better* decisions?

RB: Most of the evidence on this is that you make better decisions when you have more energy.

What happens when people are in this depleted state where their willpower is down is that they start to take shortcuts—like using one criterion instead of two or if there's a lot of information they'll uncritically weigh them all equally rather than saying, "*Those things should be irrelevant and I should really decide based on these.*" There's also "status quo bias" when people are in a relatively depleted state—they decide not to decide just letting things ride, or they postpone decisions. Compromise is something that's also characteristically reduced when people are depleted—compromise is often a good decision.

So it does look like energy facilitates good decisions, it's just a little harder to objectively determine because you need criteria for what exactly "a good decision" is and, that's difficult to do for a lot of decisions.

On the energy issue, that took some evolving. Initially, we were using it—as Freud had—as a metaphor, the "psychological energy" concept. I didn't know if actually tying that into the body's energy made sense or not: I had always hesitated trying to say that, but a couple of odd experiments that turned up in unusual ways influenced my thinking there.

There was one where we gave people ice cream after they were depleted between the two self-control tests—the theory was if resisting temptation depletes your will power, maybe giving into temptation will increase your willpower.

It would have made us very popular if it were true—we jokingly called it the *Mardi Gras Theory* because you'd have Mardi Gras before Lent when you'd go out and drink and carouse in order to enable you to successfully meet the sacrifices required of Lent.

So we depleted people on the first self-control task and then gave them a bowl of ice cream before sending them on to the second one.

And they did do better, but one of the control conditions was that we sometimes had them eat something that *didn't* taste good but that **also** made them do better, so the *Mardi Gras Theory* was wrong because it wasn't about giving into temptation—they didn't like that stuff at all—but it worked just the same.

I had a graduate student who was upset that the study didn't work, but I said, "*Well, wait a minute,* **something** *happened there: you did counteract the effect in both conditions*", and so we got to thinking that if it wasn't the pleasure, it could actually be the calories.

We'd been talking so much about energy, could it actually be the energy from the food that matters most? So that was the point where we started reading up on glucose and energy processes in the body and so on.

That's a complicated link—clearly glucose is part of the story and we don't know if we have it all figured out yet—but that was a big move to start thinking in terms of physical energy.

Hence, you're right in what you were suggesting before: if you want to make good decisions, you should get enough sleep and eat properly and so forth so that your body's energy supply is in good shape because our ability to make good decisions is tied to that.

It's linked to the immune system: when you're fighting a cold, your body's taking all the energy it can for that, so your decisions will not be as good. And you might think, "*Well, I'm just fighting a cold, I can just go in take a test or do whatever it is I'm assigned to do*," but the reality is that you won't do it as well.

I used to push myself to keep working whenever I got sick. The doctor would tell me, "*Go drink fluids, take it easy and don't work*". But I figured that I wasn't out in the hot sun digging ditches: I'm just sitting at a desk working at the computer, that shouldn't be a problem—but I realized that, if you do that, you're starving your immune system of the energy it needs and so you stay sick for longer. The work I did during those times was generally of poor quality anyway, so now, if I start to get sick, I just try to detach from everything and go and really lie down in bed and sleep for 36 hours.

And if you do that, you can usually avoid getting sicker—it turns out to be the most efficient thing in the long run even though it might go against the grain a bit.

HB: So it's an investment in your future energy and decision-making processes—and, of course, your overall health.

RB: Yes, that's right.

HB: Have you done studies that have more rigorously quantified the associated energy involved? You pointed out that in the study with the ice cream and the other food that didn't taste very good they were roughly equivalent in terms of calories and so the effect was the same—it wasn't related to whether people were happy about whether they were having ice cream, it was really the energy intake that they were having.

I could imagine trying to repeat an experiment like that except you would give some people twice as much energy—in whatever form, it wouldn't really matter—and somebody else half as much and, somehow, be able to measure these things.

Let me try to be a little bit clearer of what I'm thinking about.

On the one hand I could imagine it being sort of like a binary situation—a simple switch between having insufficient or sufficient energy in order to do the task at hand sufficiently well.

On the other hand, I could also envision a whole spectrum of relevant possible energies with all sorts of shades of grey—say, you'd be, on average, making some percentage of better decisions with twice as much energy as with half as much.

RB: Yes: I've not done as much work on that. We had a couple studies touching on some of that sort of thing in one of our big, early papers, and the editor didn't like that one as much as the others and told me, "*If you take that out, we'll publish the rest*"—so, of course, you always take that deal.

But my sense of the situation is that when you're fully charged, getting more glucose or energy or what have you, doesn't do any good, but after that there's a continuum of how depleted you can be.

In our current work we're comparing when people are just a little bit depleted—they've used some of their willpower—versus if they've done a whole lot and they're really wiped out; and those are somewhat different states.

That suggests that how much input—ice cream or glucose or whatever—you would need to get back to zero would be different depending on how depleted you are.

HB: Perhaps, at some point you might be able to have some kind of theory of putting some limits on how much energy various choices actually take. I'm not so much thinking of itemizing things to the millicalorie or whatever, but simply being able to say something like, *"Well, decisions like these, in this particular equivalence class, they typically take this amount of energy, and so you would need to rescue your depletion rate by such and such energy before going forwards."* Do you understand what I'm saying?

RB: Yes. I don't think the decision area has enough of a framework, really, to give a taxonomy of decisions where we can say, *"The more complicated ones will take more energy"*, but we've found instances when there's an obvious right answer or best choice which doesn't seem to deplete people as much. But developing a more general formal set of criteria to assess the type of decision that is required is naturally much more complicated.

Also, when you're choosing between options, how much you miss the things you're not getting in the ones you didn't choose seems to be a big factor in how depleted people get.

Say you're choosing between two cars and one has a colour that you like but the other is better in other respects, so you'll have some depletion from missing that colour, and if it had another unique feature that you don't get with the otherwise superior model then you'd have more depletion still.

HB: What about other factors, like the time of day? Do you have a certain time of the day when you, personally, now opt for making more significant decisions?

RB: Well, no, I guess would be the short answer, except I know not to do it when I'm wiped out or at the end of a long, difficult day, so I have become a little bit sensitive to that.

I do make more of an effort now, with a tough decision to make, to look at all the information and take it in without trying to make a decision right away and then let it go, sleep on it for a while, let my unconscious mind work on it and then come back again later when I'm reasonably fresh and face the decision and make the choice then. I think that's the best way.

There are morning people and evening people, however, and that's probably based on the difference in your biological clock. I've always been a "long clock" or evening person. I would like there to be a 27 or 28-hour day, not just so that I could get more done, but also because that would personally suit me. They say that as you get older, your clock gets shorter and you start falling asleep earlier and waking up earlier, but I'm still waiting for that to kick in—that would be helpful.

If you're an evening person, then you do have more energy in the evening, and unless you've knocked yourself out all day, that's when it would be a better time. Other people are morning people and that's when they have their best energy, so there's a best time for each individual that isn't the same as for others, which naturally interacts with how many demands have drained your willpower throughout the day.

Questions for Discussion:

1. To what extent has reading this chapter influenced how you're going to make important decisions going forward? Are there some specific ways that you believe you should modify your current decision-making behaviour?

2. Might some people have different "energy thresholds" for willpower and decision-making than others? Could such thresholds vary in a given individual throughout his lifespan? What impact might medication or behavioural therapies have on the amount of energy required to do certain tasks?

IV. A Philosophical Digression
Mind, brain, and the difference between them

HB: You mentioned your "unconscious mind," just now. What do you think the unconscious actually is and how much of a role do you think it has in many of the decisions that we make?

RB: Well, there's been a huge change. As I mentioned earlier, I started studying Freud long ago; and for him the unconscious was this kind of "dungeon of dangerous thoughts" that are banished from consciousness and lurking in the shadows—wicked desires and all of that. Nowadays, the general picture people have of your unconscious is more like your "support staff", working behind the scenes efficiently and helping you get things done.

We have to recognize that consciousness is probably a late evolutionary product, and lots of stuff is going on in the brain and in the mind—and only a little bit of it is conscious.

Some people think that consciousness doesn't do that much and that it's just, sort of, riding along and enjoying the show, but I'm rather sceptical that nature would have gone through all the trouble of creating consciousness just to have a spectator. I think it's because there are things you can *only do* in consciousness. I put it once that consciousness is a place where the unconscious mind can construct meaningful sequences of thought.

The unconscious can learn specific ideas and associations—it's really good at fast things—but sentences, paragraphs and telling stories, for example, which is such a big part of being a human being, all come from being conscious: no one tells a story unconsciously.

Indeed, to talk you have to be aware of what you're saying—it's very hard to talk while you're actually doing something else in your mind.

HB: I can imagine, but if the unconscious is a "support staff," as you just said, then it's just part of, it seems to me, this neuropsychological stuff that I have. After all, there are all sorts of things that I can't precisely identify that are going on in my particular brain—I might call it "unconscious", or "instinct", or some collection of neural firings or whatever.

So let me try to take a concrete example. I can reach out and choose one book versus another but "I"—broadly defined as what we all mean by "my conscious self"—decide to pick, say, the book on the left.

Meanwhile, there are all sorts of things I'm unconscious about—like regulating my heart, for example, as well as a number of other physiological goings on—which seem quite different and related to this idea of the unconscious as a sort of "support staff" to enable things like free will and consciousness in the normal way we describe them. Is that fair?

RB: What was the link to free will?

HB: That's a good point. I didn't precisely make the correspondence.

RB: Perhaps I could say it. Remember, the unconscious can pretty much run the show—behaviour happens all the time in other animals even without consciousness in the fully-human sense—so we could probably function, to some degree, without that much consciousness. But consciousness gives us the ability to do other things.

Animals eat, sleep, reproduce, run around and do all of those things, but animal societies don't think of other ways to do things—they haven't developed a global economy or redefined gender roles or switched to democracy from alpha male organization or anything like that. It's things like that where consciousness becomes important.

HB: Maybe I'm getting confused by this because, when you start talking about societies, that's a whole different issue. When we start talking about consciousness, I'm not sure, quite frankly, that my dog does not have consciousness—it depends on what we actually mean by consciousness. I don't at all believe, for example, like Descartes famously did, that my dog is some kind of automaton.

RB: When it comes to consciousness theories, there are two levels. There are the ones that we have in common with lots of other animals and the ones that are uniquely human.

The simple version—the "lower level," if you will—is the one that corresponds to squirrels, dogs and other animals: there's an experiencing agent that will make simple choices. It feels pain and pleasure and all the rest of that. That much came fairly early in evolution and we would call that just simple awareness.

On the other hand, consciousness would be all the other things that humans have that those creatures don't—symbolic awareness, reflective knowledge of self, language and so forth.

Language is an interesting one—I struggled with that for a while—because the unconscious clearly has language—you can flash a subliminal word and so on—but it doesn't combine them. You can't flash a sentence or even a series of words that become a sentence because the unconscious doesn't really get that.

Tony Greenwald, at University of Washington, says he's been following the priming literature for years and there's not a single study that passes what he calls the "two-word test," to prime two words.

So you can prime "green" and the unconscious thinks, *Okay, green is good,* and then prime "red" so it thinks, *Okay, red is good.* And then if you give it "green-red" it thinks, *That's a double good.*

But it takes the conscious mind to think, *Well, I don't know about green-red, that's not a simple combination of those two.* So the unconscious can do words, but to get sentences and paragraphs and all the rest of that it needs to put them together in consciousness.

HB: If I'm a neurobiologist and I hear you saying this, I might say something like, "*Okay, you're using these terms 'conscious' and 'unconscious' and I have an intuitive human understanding of these things—there are things that I do that I'm not aware of; my mind can wander, I can sometimes scan words on a page, I can do all sorts of things when I'm not fully cognizant of what it is that I'm doing—there might be some subliminal advertisement which can somehow affect my behaviour—but as a neurobiologist, if I have to draw the line and ask myself what the difference between conscious and unconscious is, then I start feeling uncomfortable because I can't actually really define this in any particular way.*"

After all, I have photons that are coming from some particular image and they're hitting my optic nerve and they're triggering various neurons here and there and there hardly seems to be a clear distinctive division between what my unconscious is as opposed to what my conscious is.

So I'm thinking that as a neurobiologist, I would have a problem with this because, while there are clearly useful heuristic distinctions in terms of awareness I understand, I have a naturally hard time understanding what they actually mean from a neurobiological perspective.

RB: They are very far from understanding that, but I suspect that most people in that profession would tell you that the brain has to do something different for a conscious versus an unconscious thought, since people think with their brains—so the difference between a conscious and unconscious thought has to be some difference in the brain activity.

It's at least produced by that; and how that happens, exactly—well, it's called the "hard problem" of consciousness—how can a physical thing produce subjective experience.

HB: OK, so maybe I should ask your view regarding what the unconscious actually *does* in terms of how it affects our behaviour. Do you think that most of our behaviour is being affected a great deal by the unconscious, by what's actually happening around us without us explicitly being aware of it?

RB: Not so much, I suspect—a lot of the processing will occur unconsciously: there's nothing that's "purely conscious" because everything in your consciousness is created by unconscious processes.

I read something recently that put this very beautifully: *The brain has no contact with the world.*

It's stuck inside this heavy, dark shell—it's cut off—and all it hears about the outside world are electrical impulses that come in here and there. So everything we think and know and do is somehow a result of this little lump of stuff getting electricity coming in—putting together our experience of, say, sitting here together and having this conversation this afternoon.

Scientists don't like the word but it's almost a miracle how this happens. So, consciousness is not a direct pipeline to reality: it is the brain making a movie that is the best guess of what's going on, and that's why it makes mistakes and so on.

There's the information coming in to your eyes, say, which is then split apart and processed in all these separate ways and then combined back together.

Where something is and *what* it is are processed separately in the brain—partly, I think, because the difference between the two eyes is really important for figuring out where it is for space but it's useless for figuring out what it is.

And then the "what it is" and "where it is" are then put back together. There are those "feature migration" experiments of people who are exposed to red squares and green triangles, but then they'll make a mistake and think that they've seen some green squares too—that's because the colour and the shape are processed separately and then put back together so that, by the time something gets into consciousness, it's been figured out.

This was a big debate early in empirical psychology when the early labs trained people to introspect and they said, "*Well, you don't really see a person or a wall or a table, you see this sensation of colour and this orientation".*

They went on and on about this and then the gestalt psychologists rebelled against this and said, "I'm not seeing 'grey shade #27'—I'm seeing a house and a tree and a car".

Well, they're *both* right, the eyes are seeing these sensations but then those are put through a lot of processing by the unconscious mind so that, by the time it shows up in consciousness, it has meaning, it is made sense of.

HB: I guess what's making me vaguely uncomfortable is that I think we look at the world a little bit differently, and so I'm trying to understand what the words are that you're using, so let me be more explicit with what I mean.

A couple of times now you've mentioned the brain when talking about how we make a decision, and it seems like you're making a clear distinction between the brain and the mind.

For me, the brain and the mind are effectively the same thing. I look at the brain as an integral part of "me" and so—exactly as you said before, with the analogy of the support staff—processes in the brain play an integral part in me making a decision to do one thing as opposed to another or to see something or feel something or move in a particular direction, and in this way I'm unconvinced that there's necessarily physical relevance to breaking something into conscious and unconscious, anymore than I see the relevance to breaking it into other scenarios where neurons are firing here as opposed to when neurons are firing there.

Now, I freely grant that I have a perception of being "aware" of some things and "not being aware" of others—of course. But at this level, I see the situation more like there is this big, detailed neurophysiological picture which represents me in totality, including things like my arm and my eyes, and at that level it's not clear why it would be helpful to make a distinction between something like the conscious and the unconscious. Do you see where I'm going with any of this?

RB: I keep thinking I see where you're going but I don't.

HB: OK, let me try to put it another way. There are people who talk about the "mind", making a distinction between the mind and the brain. There are also people who believe that there is no distinction between the mind and the brain and that the mind is just a manifestation of the brain, specifically brain states. I'm one of those people. And so it's not clear to me that the language which is being invoked to describe the mind in its various manifestations is necessarily helpful in a fundamental sense—that is, in anything other than a heuristic sense. In other words, I'm not sure exactly what you're getting, scientifically-speaking, from making those distinctions.

RB: What confuses me in your argument is that you're saying that there's no point in distinguishing conscious from unconscious and yet you're conceding that you know that something is happening in your brain when that happens.

HB: Sure. But there are lots of things that are happening in my brain that I'm not aware of, and lots of things that are not terribly well understood by anyone right now, and might never be.

So maybe I should back up. First of all, I'm not making an argument as such—in the first place, I'm not trying to convince anyone of anything, but simply trying to get a clear sense of what you believe and understand how it's different than what I believe, or at least what someone who is sympathetic to my position believes. So let me try again, because I've probably not been very clear. I believe that the mind is a manifestation of the brain.

RB: Well, if it's a manifestation of the brain, then you're not saying it's the same thing.

HB: OK, well it seems to me that to try to answer that I would have to get into aspects of what it means to cause something and what it means to exist and all of that. I guess all I'm saying is that what

I mean by "me" as a conscious being is solely a product of what's actually happening in my brain–

RB: Well, that clearly could not be true.

HB: Why not?

RB: The brain, in turn, is reacting to what's happening out in the world.

HB: Oh, sure—I'm not saying my brain is sealed off from everything like some black box—obviously there's stuff coming in and it's getting signals and all the rest of that.

RB: That adds a lot. I used to believe the same thing that you do but what kind of got me—I concede that everything that happens in your mind corresponds with something happening in the brain, but there is a higher level that is more meaningful.

What happens in the brain is electrical activity and chemical reactions, but understanding a Shakespearean sonnet involves symbolic meanings and other things that are not, themselves, purely physical, although they are represented by physical processes.

It's like the difference between a television set, being the brain, and the program that it's playing, which would be the experience—you only see the program because of what's going on and everything you see on the screen is a product of what happens inside the TV set.

However, that doesn't mean that President Obama is really nothing more than electrical activity inside the TV set: there is a real President Obama and a real TV station filming him and transmitting that, just as the brain—representing the TV set—is processing that symbolic information.

HB: OK, so I'd like to leave Obama out of this because we've already discussed his wardrobe and brought him into too many things, but let me take your sonnet example.

Clearly, there are incredibly complicated processes that go on in our brains, and I think one can impose some sort of hierarchy in terms of their inherent neuronal complexity and our consequent ability to extract meaning from them.

I'm guessing that it's relatively easy for us to have some sense of what's happening in my brain, say, when I'm looking at your jacket and how I'm measuring it as the particular colours, shapes and space—that's complicated, yes, but we can have some sort of structure.

Meanwhile, biologically interpreting my level of appreciation of a Shakespearean sonnet is vastly more complicated, I would imagine, in terms of its ability to be assessed in terms of all the relevant neural firings, but I'm unconvinced that it's a matter of kind rather than a matter of degree.

Anyway, perhaps we've reached an impasse—I'm naturally keen to talk about some other things as well—but my position is simply that what I believe myself to be, what I believe my "conscious being" to be, is simply a manifestation of the stuff in my brain, together with its interaction with the surrounding environment.

And my sense of what you're saying is something like, "*I used to believe that too, but now I think that there's more going on*", and I'm having a hard time understanding what that "more going on" actually is.

RB: Well, you just went along with me when you said, "*It's more than the brain, it's the environment and the interactions with it*".

HB: The brain certainly interacts with the environment—no problem there, whatsoever. You had me at hello, as they say.

Again, we can probably drop this, but I just brought it up—I think; it's getting hard to remember now—because I was trying to get an understanding of what, if I'm a neurobiologist, the utility might be of making this distinction between "unconscious" and "conscious."

Again, I see that, heuristically and empirically, we can certainly evaluate when people report, "*I didn't have an awareness of doing this*", or "*I did have an awareness of doing that*"—and maybe that might be useful—or maybe not—to predict behaviour.

But I'm wondering if the distinction between conscious and unconscious has any, let's say, "absolute meaning" to it, I'm wondering if it has any, as the philosophers would say, "ontological status", because I have a hard time understanding why it would.

RB: I'm tempted, as a sidelight, to make you go back and restate that last question in purely physicalistic terms in terms of brain activities and then you'll see how–

HB: Sure, but just because something is complicated doesn't mean it's impossible. There are so many things that I can't even begin to comprehend how I would do—I'm not a neurobiologist, after all, despite all my pretences to the contrary. Maybe it's even, for some physical reasons, *in principle*, impossible—though I don't know what those physical reasons would be. Just because something is difficult, in principle, doesn't mean that it's impossible.

RB: That's true but it could be. Either way, you can see the difficulty, certainly, to simply say that, "*Mind is nothing more than brain*", and then you want to ask a question about whether it's meaningful to make a distinction and so on.

Even using the word "meaningful" is not a "brain word"—and this gets us to a topic that is actually quite close to my heart, which is the reality of meaning. I have, very reluctantly, come to think that to understand reality—especially a psychological reality—we need to understand both physical processes and "meaning" as essentially non-physical relationships.

The relationship between, say, the flag of France and France is not a physical connection like the molecules of France are exerting influence on it: it's a symbolic connection.

It's easiest, perhaps, to see this sort of thing with mathematics: 7x8=56 and it always did long before there were humans with brains good enough to figure it out. It's not culturally relative: every culture that learns multiplication gets the same answers and there are some that haven't figured it out but, when they do figure it out, they will get the same answer—it's objectively there. It's just not a physical reality, it's a set of abstract relationships that the physical brain evolved to be able to use and incorporate so as to improve its survival and reproduction.

HB: OK, I hadn't expected things to move off in this direction, but it's most agreeable that they have, because, among other things, we now find ourselves in complete agreement. I think. But just to check: the claim I think you're making is that, independent of whether or not the physical brain evolved to be able to understand it, 7x8=56, period. So, in a possible world where there are no physical brains around to care, 7x8 would *still* equal 56.

RB: I would think so, yes, but it wouldn't have any effect on anything.

HB: Well, not on us if we didn't get there. So I'm guessing that you are bringing in this mathematical Platonist argument in order to argue by extension there is some level of objective meaning in things like the flag of France and France—that there are these relations that exist out of space and time somehow.

RB: It goes with the idea that all languages basically have the same concepts: just different words for them. They might slice it a little differently here and there but translation is very effective and there are very few thoughts that cannot be expressed in one language.
    This suggests that there's a universe of concepts that all these thousands of languages, all over the world, invented to say pretty much the same thing: *"It's raining"*, *"I'm hungry,"* *"My child is sick"*, *"Let's go have sex"*, *"There's danger"*, or what have you.

HB: OK, but that could be human-dependent, of course (unlike your mathematics example you gave a moment ago): that there's something in the human brain which predisposes us to use language in a particular way, maybe even in an "identical way", if we're clever enough to realize what "identical" means.

RB: It would have been better if that had carried a little farther—it would have been easier for us to be on the same page linguistically—but apparently nature couldn't quite put the language in.

Instead, the brain is really well-designed to learn language, wherever and whenever it is presented with the opportunity to do so, and there are several different kinds of grammatical structures and so on, but in the meantime the different forms of expression make it hard for us to recognize shared meaning.

But with respect to our interest in meaning in life, life is a physical event and physical process, while meaning is not physical, so trying to understand meaning through a physical process is difficult because you're using oranges to understand apples, or something like that.

And for me this is directly relevant to the question of distinguishing brain from mind. I'm certainly in agreement that everything that happens in the mind is based on something that happens in the brain, it's just that the brain is working with other stuff too, including meanings and non-physical relationships.

Again for me this is represented by the analogy I used before about how the TV set shows a program, which is in some sense distinct from the actual transistors and what not inside the actual TV set, even though they are producing it.

I see the brain and mind relationship in the same way—nothing happens on the TV screen that isn't a result of what's going on inside the television set; and, in the same way, nothing happens in our mind that isn't produced by neural activity.

Questions for Discussion:

1. Do you agree or disagree with Roy when he says, "All languages basically have the same concepts: just different words for them"? Those interested in related discussions on this topic are referred to Chapter 8 of **Babbling Barbarians: How Translators Keep Us Civilized** with translator David Bellos and Chapter 10 of **Sign Language Linguistics** with linguist Carol Padden.

2. Are you convinced by the analogy Roy invokes of the TV set and the TV program? Can we objectively distinguish between the two in all cases? Often this analogy is expressed in term of a "hardware vs. software" divide. Readers interested in related perspectives on this issue are referred to Chapters 10-12 of **Speaking and Thinking** with psychologist Victor Ferreira, as well as Chapters 2, 8 and 9 of **Philosophy of Brain** with philosopher Patricia Churchland.

3. To what extent are the two "vision processing streams" that Roy mentions in this chapter necessarily linked to his view of consciousness? For more information on the details of these processing streams see Chapter 3 of **Vision and Perception** with neuroscientist Kalanit Grill-Spector.

4. What is mathematical Platonism, and to what extent do you think it is relevant to this discussion? Readers interested in this topic are referred to Chapter 1 of **Pushing the Boundaries** with scientific polymath Freeman Dyson, as well as the entire Ideas Roadshow conversation **Plato's Heaven: A User's Guide** with philosopher James Robert Brown.

V. Free Will

Incorporating cultural factors into our decision-making

HB: So perhaps it's time now to move on to discuss free will. So let me say what I mean by that and you should obviously feel free to give your own interpretation or tell me where your thoughts differ from any of this.

So what I mean by "free will," is that the idea that I, as an individual agent, am sufficiently autonomous as to have it in my power to be able to generally choose one action over another in any given instance.

My understanding is that there has been some research into social conditioning and social factors that would be operating behind the scenes impinging upon my choices to the extent where I may not even be aware of the fact that I don't actually have complete autonomy in making those individual choices.

Some people believe that, resulting from a combination of various different cultural factors, while I might *think* that I can choose whatever I want, actually, I'm predisposed towards one particular choice rather than another particular choice.

RB: Yes, I think the idea of complete freedom, that's probably an ideal. The philosophers like to debate the question of free will as if it's yes or no: *Do people have it or not?*

In psychology, most things are on a continuum, so some acts are freer than others but is the unconscious contributing? Well, everything that happens in consciousness is a result of the unconscious, so yes. Can there be things that influence your decision that you're not aware of? Yes, there can be. Can you think you have made a free choice when you're actually tricked or primed? Yes, you can.

To me, the requirement that it be complete or absolute—if you insist that free will has to be of that form—then there's probably not going to be anything that meets that criterion.

But the difference between freer and less free—people know that difference in their daily lives, they see it in others—it is something that really happens. To me, the crucial thing is that the world around us often consists of multiple possibilities and evolution gave us the ability to choose between them.

The beginnings of this go back to, probably, plants versus animals: plants don't make decisions, they pretty much—even when something comes over to eat them—stand still, whereas animals move out of the way if something comes over to eat them. The animal has to have a central nervous system and a brain because it has to get it all coordinated. It makes choices: the purpose of that brain is to prolong the life of the animal that houses it.

The beginnings of the central nervous system are movement—locomotion—and eating. So the very earliest beginnings for central decision-making are moving around to find food.

Free will, to the extent that we believe in the term, would be an advanced—in the evolutionary sense—human form of this. Instead of just making decisions in the physical world like, *Am I going to climb this tree or that tree to look for some food?* you have symbolic decisions like, say, *I promised to pay my mortgage every month* or *I'll pay my taxes* or *I'll take care of my spouse and marriage*—these incorporate a lot of meaning for functioning in the cultural systems where we live.

The key difference, the foundation of my thinking in the last ten years, has been that the distinctively human traits are adaptations to make culture possible.

Like all other animals, we have to solve the problems of survival and reproduction. You need a biological strategy—every living thing has some strategy for doing that—but ours is a very unusual one as human beings: we create these complex social systems with meaning, with shared information, with interlocking roles and identities and moral obligations and so forth, all of which works very well for us. As a result, we live a lot better than most other creatures, but it needs a lot more psychological capabilities to successfully function in a culture.

So the traits that define us as human—and that's not *all* the traits, we share many with other animals—the ones that set us apart are evolutionary adaptations to make possible this new strategy of living in a civilized culture.

HB: That all sounds completely reasonable to me, but I'll be honest with you, I get frustrated when I hear people talk about free will because I have a different sense of what the free will argument actually is.

It seems to me that what you're saying is that there's no such thing as complete, unfettered free will in the sense that we are being subtly or not so subtly influenced all over the place for all aspects of our behaviour—some of them we're aware of and some of them we may not be aware of.

RB: Yes, it's always situated, it's always fettered.

HB: Right; and insofar as we're not always aware of what may be impinging on our decision process, we're not completely free.

This strikes me as a very different discussion than the debate about whether there's an inherently deterministic universe and, as material beings that are subjected to those deterministic laws, to what extent our actions are predetermined according to some super-duper algorithm in the sky which might well be impenetrable to us, but nonetheless exists. And then people start waving their hands around and talking about quantum mechanics and so forth and it all gets very opaque and very muddled very quickly.

But that's not what you're talking about, thank goodness. So let me ask you a different question. Do people argue with you about what you just expressed to me?

RB: About evolution for culture? Well, it's not a widely shared view, although, when I bring it up, it does seem to persuade people. Because the influence of evolutionary theory has been so strong, there's been a tendency in social psychology to put a lot of emphasis on being social animals and what we have in common with other animals rather than what sets us apart and makes us different. So that's been one thing that I've been emphasizing.

HB: I see, so those holding a contrary view would invoke some sort of evolutionary continuum, demanding why should we draw the line at humans? Is that the argument?

RB: Well, it's not so much a rigorous philosophical position, it's more a conviction that we're social animals. They say things like, *"Why do we help other people? We help our close relatives more than our friends and our friends more than strangers"*, or, *"Who would you run for to save in a burning building? Well, if it's between your mother or your high school track coach, you'd go in and get your mother."*

And then they'd say, *"Well, look, we're just like other animals because they help kin"*, but I think we need to pay more attention to the fact that humans will help total strangers—they will donate money to fight disease or reduce poverty in other parts of the world with people who don't know us or look like us or will never hear of us or be grateful.

HB: So effectively what you seem to be saying is something like, "Look around you, look at all the structures that have been built by humans, look at the levels of integration throughout society, look at all these structures that have been built through cooperation, collaboration and culture.

RB: Yes. Now, returning to the free will debate, I've been listening to these arguments for a couple of years now and there are actually three different arguments I think people are having.

The first is causality—some people think determinism is just causality and that free will means some kind of exemption from causality. I don't really find that all that persuasive. To me, there are so many different kinds of causes already, and free will would just be another kind of cause—there's no exemption from causality.

The second is reductionism: *Can everything at a higher level be explained by what happens at a lower level?* and *Are we just biological organisms with brains, which are, in turn, just chemical reactions, which are, in turn, just physicals processes of atoms and molecules?* And there, I think the weight of scientific opinion is the answer, *No, at each level, new kinds of causes come into play*—if you want to study love at the level of gravity—

HB: Well, gravity is an attractive force.

RB: Good one. Anyway, I believe that all the relevant aspects of instinct disappear as you get down to those lower levels. Of course they are influenced by them and they have to work through them—nothing can violate the laws of physics—but a lot of things happen that those laws of physics are not going to explain just by themselves.

So, in human terms, the psychology of a person verses the activity of a brain—well, you can't do anything without your brain but there is much more than that if you want to incorporate meaning and understanding the social system, the culture, the economy, the political structure and so forth. And that's not all in the brain, although the brain is helping your body participate in that. So, reductionism is the second objection, and I'm opposed to that in the way I just described.

And the last objection concerns the original meaning of determinism, which is that there's only one possible future: that's the predestination debate.

To me, if you embrace that then that is incompatible with free will, but often the way people argue it is that, somehow, there has to be something in *you* that can create different, possible outcomes out there—but I think that's backwards. I think that the outcomes, the different possibilities are already out there and so nature gave us the capacity to choose among them. That's analogous to an animal who can choose to go one way or another so as to get food better.

One thing I've been doing research on recently is how people think about the future and determinism would be completely useless: to tell people that what they're going to have for dinner tomorrow or whom they're going to marry is actually all inevitable—it's been determined since the Big Bang—doesn't really help the person at all: they still have to make the decision.

The fact is that the future presents itself as a matrix of possibilities—with some constraints and dangers and opportunities and other things—and these things are possible but not definite.

That's why we have an agent inside us to make choices to try to produce the outcome that's better for us than the outcome that's worse for us.

So, again, we see this in squirrels and dogs and so on but, in the human being, it's processing meaning in the sense of morality and economics and cultural symbolism and legal obligations and all these other things. And all of that is the "2.0 version" of the chipmunk choosing whether to run up this tree or that tree.

Questions for Discussion:

1. To what extent is evolutionary theory incompatible with determinism?

2. Why does Roy invoke the notion of reductionism when describing possible objections to his views? Is it possible to be a "strict reductionist" and still believe in free will? Readers with an interest in more generally exploring the philosophical aspects of reductionism and its limitations are referred to Chapter 4 of **Minds and Machines** with neuroscientist Miguel Nicolelis and Chapter 7 of **The Problems of Physics, Reconsidered** with physicist Tony Leggett.

3. Might it be countered that other animals also form cultural structures and that human structures differ from these by a matter of degree rather than kind?

4. How is a dog choosing a cookie that happens to be shaped like one he is familiar with different in principle from a person being influenced by someone who looks like one of their favourite musicians?

VI. Cultural Distinctiveness
And its relevance

HB: Tell me a little bit more about the research into the future that you just alluded to. What specifically are you imagining and what sort of experiments have you done and might do later?

RB: It started with my friend Marty Seligman who was writing an essay and he said to me, *"You know, psychology tends to explain behaviour based on what happened in the past, but when I do stuff, I do it based on the future."*

The big traditional theories in psychology were Freudian psychoanalysis—your adult self as a product of what happened in your childhood experiences—and the notion of reinforcement history—rats learning from priori experiences, say—both of which interpret what you're doing now as a result of the past.

But he said, *"You know, for me there's really a lot more emphasis on the future."* So I got interested in this, and we wrote a paper with a couple of philosophers, and then he managed to get a big grant to support other research there.

HB: This grant has actually arrived? It's not in the future?

RB: Yes, the grant has actually arrived—some of it lies in the future and some lies in the past.

We didn't know how much people think about the future, so we've just done this giant study where we used people's mobile phones like a beeper; every so often, it would beep, and they'd have to stop and say, *"Okay, what were you thinking about just when the beep went off? What was the last thought you had? Was it about past, present, future or none of the above or all of the above?"*

HB: So you get a real sense of how preoccupied people are about the future.

RB: Yes; and what correlates with it. You get a ton of data with this, so we've been struggling to analyze it, but **emotion**, for example, in terms of happiness, is highest when you're focused in the present: the more you move into the past or the future, the worse you'll feel. **Meaning**, however, is the other way around: it's higher into the past and future and meaning—in particular, connects across time.

HB: Hold on, I've lost you. Tell me what you mean by "meaning" with respect to the past and the future.

RB: Well, we had people rate how meaningful their thoughts were when the buzzer went off.

HB: So, their thoughts that are based in the past and future are valued higher in terms of meaningfulness?

RB: Yes, they're rated as higher in meaning, they're more meaningful, especially when they checked all three. So the highest, most meaningful thoughts, on average, were the ones where they checked past, present and future. Present and future was a particularly important category and those were also highly meaningful. If it was just past, present or future by themselves, it's less meaningful yet; and if there was no time at all, then it was the least meaningful.

HB: You said that there's a ton of data. When you do these experiments, do you do them across the United States or internationally or what? I ask because I could imagine that there would be some cultural factors that would come into play as well.

RB: Yes. Well, it's a tremendous job to run one of these things. This particular study we ran in Chicago, because the lead guy, Wilhelm

Hofmann, was at the University of Chicago—he had the software and he was able to get it done with something like 500 people in the city of Chicago over the course of about three days.

The previous one we had done was on desire, and we had done that one in Germany because he had been there at the University of Würzburg, so we had 200 Germans at that point.

And you're right: if we could somehow do it in rural Africa or a war zone in the Middle East or something then that would possibly bring in some other dimensions, but the practical constraints are very formidable.

HB: I can imagine that this would be a common concern for you in many different areas of social psychology. If you're trying to look at social and cultural influences on humans, then there's presumably always a desire to make sure you're painting as wide a picture as you possibly can in terms of different human societies and correspondingly different pressures. Presumably it might well be that you will encounter local effects that will overshadow a more general phenomenon that you're looking for.

RB: Yes, there's periodic concern about that, especially because, broadly three-quarters of the studies are done at universities with students just because they happen to be there and have time to be in the experiments, so it's a sample of convenience.

People periodically get all worried about this because we're somehow not studying "real people"—as if students aren't real people—and they go out and look out in the "real" world and things mostly turn out the same with a different kind of sample.

Now, we don't have a lot of, say, going into the wilds of Papua New Guinea or anything. The effects might be larger or smaller, there might be different ways of dealing with them, but basic effects like you're more likely to act aggressively if I insult you than if I praise you—well, that's probably true everywhere. Again, the amount of aggression might vary, but it's very rarely going to flip so that it's the other way around and people attack people who praise them and not criticize them.

So a lot of the things will be true, but I think it is something that we always have to be on guard for. In science you always have to be careful not to overgeneralize.

The question of how big cultural differences are is, itself, a profound and somewhat controversial one. Cultural anthropologists in particular, have career goals that are set up to reinforce the idea that you're going to find something different in different places; and so the whole ethos in the field is that every culture is different and that cultures can make people act in totally different ways.

I remember one anthropologist saying to me, "*If you're an anthropologist and you've got a grant and you spent two years out in the field with this tribe and came back and wrote a report that said,* **'Well, they're pretty much like everybody else'**—

HB: You wouldn't get another grant very quickly.

RB: That's right: you wouldn't get another grant for a long time.

So there's a structural push to find something unique and special about them, which naturally leads to the difference among cultures being overstated. I've seen how far it's come down since I was a student: there was this total, widespread belief in cultural relativism to the point that you just couldn't understand what it was like for someone to be in love in, say, an Asian culture.

Nowadays, most of us appreciate that they might have a few other wrinkles or complications that we don't have, but it's not all that different from our situation.

There have also been times when people were explicitly ignoring cultural differences and others would rise up and say, "*No, there really are some cultural differences*", but I think the emphasis has now been on identifying a few big key ones rather than to assume that every culture is so different that you can't generalize from one to another.

HB: And then presumably examining the specific impact of what those key ones might happen to be under the overarching assumption that we are all, at some level, basically the same.

RB: Yes. I'm very interested in culture, but I'm not interested in the differences in culture so much as the similarities because I'm looking for human nature, so I kind of want to see the things that are in common among all cultures—well, all is too much for social science but say in over 90-95%. To me, in many cases cultural differences represent different solutions to the same basic problems.

As Marvin Harris and the cultural materialists said, "*Whatever else cultures do, they have to provide structures so that people can eat and sleep and have babies and take care of themselves in various ways*"—in other words, the original, basic function of culture is to provide the basic, material conditions of life. You can solve them in different ways, like with sexual morals: everybody can have sex with anybody all the time or you can only have sex with the person you're married to—one person in your life—or you have something else, something in between.

There's no perfect system but it helps to have everybody agreeing on the same values, because once the culture disagrees about its values, it's harder to get things done. Take something as simple as cars: you can drive on the right, you can drive on the left, it doesn't matter as long as everyone else is doing the same thing—the agreement, in a way, matters more. They are different solutions to the same basic problem.

Questions for Discussion:

1. Do you agree that thoughts that you consider the most meaningful tend to connect across time and involve the past, present and future?

2. Are all human cultures equivalent at some level? If not, how can they be objectively distinguished without invoking a measuring system that is itself culturally biased?

VII. Numbed By Rejection
More than just a metaphor

HB: Suppose I were an omniscient being and I could answer any scientific questions that you might have, what would they be?

RB: I would like to learn more about the details of the relationship of mind to body involving some of the things we've talked about earlier, like willpower and how it's tied into glucose and adenosine and other processes, and how, ultimately, does inanimate activity of our chemicals in the brain produce the subject of experience of consciousness? That would be one that I'd like to know.

There are other things I'm curious about. There are questions with direct policy implications that arose when I was working on the sex literature, such as, *Does pornography increase desire or does it satisfy desire?* It's particularly relevant, as has been pointed out, with sex offenders such as pedophiles. If it turns out to reduce desire than it might be possible to make virtual pornography and thereby help protect potential victims. I don't know the answer to that, but I'd be curious to know; and I think it would be better to know that one way or the other.

My third one would be that I'd like to have a good account of the emergence of social organization up through and including economic and political organization. There are some very impressive books on that I've been reading, but it's a big problem to put it all together and figure out how it all happens, so I'd really like to get a grasp on that.

In a sense, this goes down to the very beginnings of how we got chemistry from physics: that matter lends itself to organization.

HB: So, this is an understanding of emergent structure at the socio-political level.

RB: Right: *How does emergence happen at the higher levels?* I'd like to understand the emergence per se and how things take on new levels of organization like, *How did we get from chemicals, which are not alive, to living things?* and *How do we get from living things to things with agency that can make choices?* and *How did we get from there to Shakespearean sonnets and the iPhone?*

HB: You had me right up until you made an equivalence between Shakespearean sonnets and the iPhone.

RB: Oh, it wasn't an equivalence, it was supposed to be the difference, that a different kind of product is standing at the apex of technological development as well as the apex of artistic creativity. The point was that I was trying to illustrate things as culminations of—

HB: I was kidding.

RB: OK. I could have used the Model T.

HB: It wouldn't have made any difference.
    Anything else? Anything I haven't asked? There are a lot of things we haven't talked about and obviously we could go on a lot longer but I don't want to take up too much of your time. Is there anything that you'd like to say that you didn't have a chance to say?

RB: Did we hit everything on your list?

HB: Well, I don't really have a list per se, but we didn't talk about *The Need To Belong*, and we didn't talk very much about human sexuality and the impact of culture, or irrational behaviour and why people do apparently self-defeating things that are not in their best interest. So if you're up for talking more, maybe you can pick one of those.

RB: Well, how about *The Need To Belong*?

HB: Sounds great. I'd like to ask one related question at the outset. I had the good fortune of talking to Barbara Fredrickson not too long ago (*The Science of Emotions*) and among other things she mentioned her work on the importance of making human connections and directly measurable physiological effects that are involved with that. So my related specific question is: Have you worked with her on any of this stuff and would you like to in the future?

RB: I would like to. I haven't worked with her because I know she's rather busy. I actually see her fairly regularly because we go to many of the same conferences and I always have an interesting conversation with her, so I've been able to keep up with what she's doing reasonably well—but no, I haven't yet done any work with her.

The thing is, at this stage, you work a lot with your graduate students and I have to take care of all mine and she works with all of hers. If some graduate student would want to work with both of us, that would certainly facilitate the process.

HB: Sounds very reasonable. So tell me more about *The Need To Belong*. How did that all happen for you and how did that work impact your understanding?

RB: Well, *The Need To Belong* was a big change in my thinking too. When I was in graduate school, I was reading a lot and trying to absorb the information from the psychological literature. There was a tendency to explain everything as basic processes happening inside the person; and I thought, *Well, maybe there's more of an interpersonal dimension going on that people are only really give lip service to—after all, it is **social** psychology.*

There were a lot of discussions of people being concerned about their self-esteem and how they'll react to failure or criticism or success as it depended on their sense of self-esteem.

And I remember thinking—and this ended up being my dissertation—*Well, maybe people are a little concerned with that but they're probably a lot **more** concerned with how **other** people esteem them.*

So we gave people praise or criticism either confidentially or publicly. The effect on the self-esteem should be the same—what it tells you about yourself is identical—but boy, they reacted much more if somebody else knew about it.

So I've been a bit of a contrarian in social psychology saying, "*We need to be more social*", and after that time, indeed, social psychology went a lot *more* inside the single mind: most of social psychology is now done by having someone sit behind a computer and make ratings, which is a very solitary activity.

HB: That's ironic.

RB: Yes, it is ironic. So I've been on this campaign to say, "*You know, people relate to **others**; a lot of things are much more interpersonal than we've assumed*". There was this general sense that, *Well, OK, people interact, but what they do and say to each other is a product of other things going on inside them.*

And I tried to turn that around and say, "*Inner processes serve interpersonal functions: what's going on inside you is there to facilitate relating to others*".

Basically, nature doesn't care what's going on inside you and what your self-esteem is or how happy you are or anything like that—it doesn't have any clear effect on your survival or reproduction.

But what *other* people think of you turns out to be absolutely crucial. For a species like ours, if others don't accept you, you're not going to survive, let alone reproduce.

I remember hearing some psychologists talking about the idea that the fear of death is the most important motivation and that drives people, which goes back to Ernest Becker and *The Denial of Death*, the Pulitzer Prize-winning book in the '60s about how humans are the only creatures who know of their own mortality.

And these social psychologists had done some experiments in support of this big theory: they were fixated on anxiety, talking about how anxiety was really all about death.

And I remember thinking, *I don't know that anxiety is really all about death. I don't have much anxiety but it's not over whether I'm going to die, it's about whether my girlfriend is going to dump me, or something like that.*

So I went out and looked at the literature and read all the anxiety research that I didn't know anything about; and, sure, there is some fear of death, but it's mostly fear of rejection and lack of belongingness.

So we published that and there were a bunch of commentaries; and when it was all done, one of the guys—Mark Leary—said to me, "*You know, you were right about anxiety, but it's more than that*".

So Mark and I wrote that paper, *The Need to Belong*. It took us several years and we tried to relate this urge to connect with others to mental processes, to emotions, to health—and over and over. It turned out that it had huge effects. The paper has now been cited in scientific literature something like 8,000 different times. It's had a really big impact on people.

It wasn't like we discovered something new, that people want to be with others—but it had always been lurking in the background of theories of human nature, and we said, "*No, this should be a central thing. It's a very strong motivation and it's one of the most fundamental things. That's why rejection is bad and why people have anxiety about that.*"

We started studying what happens when that need is thwarted, and we did a lot of research on what happens when we reject people.

In the lab we can't do anything comparable to, say, getting a divorce or being turned down by the medical school you wanted to go to, but people react very strongly even to being rejected by somebody they just met in the lab. You talk to someone for a few minutes and then that person doesn't want to interact with you anymore and that produced *big* effects on cognition.

We'd give them an intelligence test after a simple rejection like that and their scores dropped by something like 25%. Something happens there: they become more aggressive, they become less helpful to others—which, if you're being rejected, you'd think you'd want to be the opposite: you should want to be more of a nice guy.

It's almost like we make ourselves be a good person based on whether or not other people are going to include us, because that's how we live as a species: we make connections. But if they're not going to include us, people figure that they're not going to bother being a good person. They even stop self-regulating—they don't change their behaviour as much.

The thing that didn't work out was that we thought being rejected would produce this wave of being upset, that everything would be mediated by a really intense distress reaction—and we just didn't find that. We found big behavioural effects but we just could never get people to say that they were really upset.

It was odd: I'd describe our procedures and people would say, "*Oh, I'd be so upset if that happened to me*". So you'd come into the lab with a group of five or six other people, and then you'd be told that we were going to pair off and everybody was told to write down two names of who you'd like to work with. And then I'd come to your cubical and say, "*Oh, nobody picked you*".

People would tell me, "*I'd start crying if that happened*", but we did that, we even measured emotion half a dozen different ways but they were feeling nothing.

What we gradually realized is that you just, sort of, go numb. Mark Leary and Geoff MacDonald had a paper surveying animal research, and they found that when animals are rejected—when baby rats are thrown out of the litter, say—they become insensitive to physical pain: there's this, sort of, analgesic reaction, probably because of a release of opioids or something like that.

HB: This ties into what I was going to ask you before. Earlier in the conversation when we were talking about energy differentials and I asked you if this would apply to other domains, might it be possible to measure pre-rejection and post-rejection in people in terms of some energy differential which would be analogous to what you did with willpower and glucose and so forth?

RB: Yes, possibly you could. There's always the question of how to measure energy. We've measured their self-control after rejection, which gets worse: although they're fully capable of it, they just don't want to bother. If you give them a sufficient reason to do so, then they'll do fine—it's not like it really takes something out of them. It gets complicated because some others can still suck it up and do well, but on the whole it looks more like they're able to but they're just not willing.

HB: There's this numbness, as you say.

RB: The numbness is a different effect that shuts down their emotion system and makes them less empathic to others. We found that rejected people will be more aggressive—they'll hurt others more and they'll help others less—and that's probably because they just don't empathize: they don't feel another's pain and they don't realize that their emotion system is shut down.

There's this thing called affective forecasting, which is whether or not people can predict their future emotional reactions—they tend to predict a much bigger reaction than they actually have.

We can do that with football games, for example, with regards to the football game next month, how happy will you be if your team wins and how unhappy if they lose? So we tried *that* after rejection—and sure enough, they didn't care.

Everybody else said, *"Oh, I'll be so happy if we win this game; and if we lose, on a 7 point scale, it will be a 1, it will be the worst thing I can imagine"*, which is hard to believe in itself. Meanwhile the rejected people for the same circumstances, were at maybe a 3 on the 7-point scale.

HB: Does this correlate across ages as well? I could imagine that people who were older who had been forced to deal with rejection more often in the past might have some of the numbness diminish as opposed to some younger people.

RB: That I don't know: we haven't gotten older people in for that one, that's more difficult. We were doing this with a pain sensitivity measure; and sure enough when you're rejected, you just don't feel the pain.

HB: Physically?

RB: Physical pain, yes. We put a little thing on them that squeezes their finger and it gradually squeezes harder and harder. You tell us when it starts to hurt and then you say when you need it to stop because it's hurting too much.

And both of those came way later after they had been rejected, as opposed to being accepted or neutral control. Rejection, somehow, just made the pain not bother people for a much longer time.

HB: Perhaps that could be used for medicinal purposes, maybe we could use that as an anaesthetic: just reject people instead.

RB: Well, Nathan DeWall, my student, came to me and said, "*Does that mean if we gave people Aspirin as a painkiller that they would be less bothered by rejection?*" and this seemed to me like the craziest idea possible, but he'd several other things work in the past and had built up some credibility, so I said "*Go ahead and try it—I'll give you the $1000 for whatever we need in terms of pills and so forth*".

So he did it; and damn it worked: people were less bothered by rejection in every day life. We had them keep a diary for a couple weeks of whether or not they had hurt feelings on each day. "Hurt feelings" is something that people will say before they're actually expressing emotional distress. And in the placebo group, it stayed high—they had hurt feelings all along. The people who were taking acetaminophen every day, after about the 9th day, they started having a significant drop in hurt feelings.

He's gone on to do more work on this at the University of Kentucky. He was tracking loneliness and had a large sample of students across the year. Not having people talk to you tends to make you lonely—except, he said, for the chronic marijuana smokers. He didn't know why that was, so he went and looked up the molecule and it was fairly similar to the acetaminophen. I know California gives medical marijuana for pain relief; and apparently it works for "social pain" as well.

HB: Again, there's this link between psychology and physiology that we keep coming back to—it's just manifesting itself in a different way this time.

RB: Exactly: we found both psychological and physiological effects. So rejection, again, goes to the core of what we're all about: you don't need everybody to love you but you need some people.

HB: Well, thank you very much Roy. That's a great point to end on.

RB: My pleasure, Howard.

Questions for Discussion:

1. What might be an evolutionary justification for the phenomenon of post-rejection numbness?

2. Might there be instances when being numb to "social pain" is disadvantageous?

3. To what extent are people, in general, more sensitive to group dynamics than most psychologists and economists typically recognize? How might this impact our understanding of a diverse range of other issues, such as voting patterns, international relations or economic cycles? Additional perspectives on this issue can be found in Chapter 5 (among others) of **Critical Situations** with psychologist Philip Zimbardo and **Improving Human Rights** with human rights expert Emilie Hafner-Burton.

Continuing the Conversation

Those interested in a deeper sense of Roy's ideas are referred to his many books, including *The Power of Bad: How the Negativity Effect Rules Us and How We Can Rule It*, *Evil: Inside Human Violence* and *Cruelty and Willpower: Rediscovering the Greatest Human Strength*.

Mindsets

Growing Your Brain

A conversation with Carol Dweck

Introduction
Justified Applause

It's hard to find a more universally accepted piece of parenting advice than the importance of regularly showering your child with praise.

From diminishing the disappointment of failure to actively rewarding achievement, consistently bestowing positive reinforcement and external support seems to be one of the paradigmatic responsibilities of parenthood, allowing children to develop the vital sense of confidence and self-esteem in their formative years that will equip them for success in later life when battling through an often indifferent and uncaring world.

Stanford University psychologist Carol Dweck believes in the power of praise as well, but for her, the issue is considerably more subtle. Depending on how you do it, she tells us, you might actually be doing more harm to your child than good.

Carol tells us that it is vital to praise children—or students, or employees, or virtually anyone—for the *effort* made in accomplishing tasks, the work required to gain conceptual understanding, rather than solely the attainment of a positive result. Doing so, she's convinced, goes a long way towards reinforcing what she calls a "growth mindset."

Those with a growth mindset see themselves as a work in progress. They understand that one's potential for achievement is not fully fixed in advance according to some innate, abstract criteria—rather, it is firmly linked to a willingness to work hard and develop.

This view, Carol hastens to point out, is not simply the latest in popular self-help, but fully supported by modern neuroscientific views of the plasticity of the brain. Through the vital process of grappling with difficult problems and the act of struggling to make progress, we actually strengthen and reinforce vital neurological connections, thereby, as she puts it, "growing our brains." Learning how to address difficult problems and master important new techniques, it turns out, literally makes us smarter.

Meanwhile, those who are mired in what she calls a "fixed mindset" believe something quite different. For them, working hard is something that only less talented (less intelligent, less gifted) people need do. This way of thinking clearly runs the risk of leading to a sense of complacency and unwillingness to push oneself. But it is actually much worse than that: those in a fixed mindset not only naturally shirk new challenges (why needlessly risk one's position at the top of the hierarchy?), they inevitably become so consumed with defending their place on the social and intellectual hierarchy that they soon entirely stop learning and developing for its own sake. Curiosity and passion naturally fall by the wayside once one becomes preoccupied with simply keeping up appearances and reputations.

In other words, all of this goes considerably beyond simply mouthing platitudes about the value of hard work. After all, those in a fixed mindset work hard too—they expend considerable effort and suffer significant amounts of stress convincing everyone that they are naturally accomplished.

It is not that they are inherently lazy or incapable of working hard. It is that their very worldview, their mindset, renders the idea of such work both distasteful and embarrassing. If working hard at mathematics, say, is something that "only stupid people do," which top-ranked mathematics student would ever want to admit to someone that such a thing is precisely what she has been doing?

Okay, you might be thinking to yourself, but what has all of this to do with praise?

Well, it turns out that telling someone, *"Wow, you got 8/10. You must be really smart,"* is a sure-fire way to reinforce a fixed mindset and lead them on the road to intellectual perdition. Meanwhile, praising people for their effort: *"Wow, you got 8/10. You must have worked really hard,"* naturally encourages them to adopt a growth mindset.

Idle speculation? Not at all. As a practicing researcher, Dweck and her colleagues were able to verify their mindset hypothesis from long hours of detailed experimental research:

> *"We conducted studies with hundreds of students, mostly early adolescents. We first gave each student a set of ten fairly difficult problems from a nonverbal IQ test. They mostly did pretty well on these and when they finished we praised them. Some were praised for their ability and some for their effort.*
>
> *"Both groups were exactly equal to begin with. But right after the praise, they began to differ. As we feared, the ability praise pushed students right into a fixed mindset: when we gave them a choice, they rejected a challenging task that they could learn from. They didn't want to do anything that could expose their flaws and call into question their talent.*
>
> *"In contrast, when students were praised for effort, 90 percent of them wanted the challenging new task they could learn from.*
>
> *"Then we gave the students some new hard problems, which they didn't do so well on. After these problems, most of the ability-praised students said it wasn't fun anymore. Meanwhile, many of the effort-praised students maintained that the hard problems were the most fun.*
>
> *"We then looked at student performance. After experiencing the difficult problems, the performance of the ability-praised students plummeted, even when we gave them some more of the easier problems. But the effort-praised kids showed better and better performance. They had used the hard problems to sharpen their skills, so that when they returned to the easier ones, they were well ahead."*

These results are intriguing not simply because they provide such a clear experimental verification of Carol's thesis, but also because they imply how easily subjects can slide from one mindset to another.

With a bit of work and understanding, Carol tells us, anyone can adopt a growth mindset and begin enthusiastically embracing challenges and personal development.

And she should know. Carol, herself, is a former "fixed-mindset person" who was launched on her road of mindset discovery by a series of serendipitous encounters with "growth-mindset children".

As she was probing the psychological phenomenon of "learned helplessness" through a series of experiments with young children, she discovered, to her amazement, some completely unexpected reactions to the intractable problems that she was giving them.

> "Some of these kids were not only able to cope with failure, they seemed to relish it. I would give them certain problems that they were incapable of solving—I called them 'the failure problems'—but one 10-year old boy would rub his hands together and smack his lips, saying, 'I love a challenge.'

> "Another one looked up and said, 'You know, I was hoping this would be informative'.

> "And some of them even wound up solving the problems that they weren't supposed to solve, because they were approaching them in such an effective way.

> "These kids had an attitude that was so foreign from my way of thinking, but on the other hand I knew that they had a secret, they had something very wise that they had figured out."

And Carol, in turn, was sensible enough to pay close attention to these "wise children" in her midst, investing increasing amounts of effort to understand what exactly was driving them and how the rest of us could successfully emulate their attitude.

The rest, as they say, is history, as Professor Dweck has become one of the most successful and influential social psychologists of our time, with her mindset work universally praised throughout the world.

Suffice it to say that it's very well-earned.

The Conversation

I. Fixed Beginnings

Mrs. Wilson's legacy

HB: Let's start right at the very beginning. What is a "mindset"?

CD: In my work, a mindset is a belief people have about whether their basic qualities are just fixed, given, inborn, or represent something that can change and develop.

For example, some people have a fixed mindset about their intellectual abilities. They think their intelligence is just fixed: you have a certain amount and that's that. What we find is that when people have this view, they don't want to do hard things that might reveal some sense of inadequacy, and they don't stick to hard things because they feel dumb.

But other people have a growth mindset. They believe their basic abilities can be developed through hard work, good strategies, and help and mentoring from others. They don't think everyone's the same, or that anyone can be Einstein, but they understand that people don't become the people that they become without effort—just as Einstein didn't become Einstein until he worked at it.

So people with a growth mindset are more likely to take on hard challenges and stick to them, because that's how you learn and grow.

HB: According to your book you also had a fixed mindset when you were younger before you began to appreciate the power of a growth mindset. Maybe you could talk a little bit about you story, because, while you occasionally refer to it throughout your book *Mindset*, you don't talk about it at great length.

CD: Well, I grew up in the heyday of the IQ, fixed-intelligence era. My sixth grade teacher seated us around the room in IQ-order and assigned all responsibilities and privileges in terms of IQ. So this was really a fixed-mindset era.

HB: Was this normal? Because it sounds almost barbaric to me that your teacher would line you up in terms of IQ. Did other students and other people you knew do this sort of thing?

CD: It wasn't typically done. She carried it to an extreme. But at that time people did place a lot of faith in the idea of IQ testing as a summary of intelligence.

Now, as I also say in my book *Mindset*, the inventor of the IQ test did not have that in mind at all. Alfred Binet had a radical growth mindset, but the Americans and the English took his test and told themselves that they were measuring intelligence, often explicitly using terms like "fixed intelligence". As with many fads, it was adopted whole-heartedly by many educators.

Mrs. Wilson was probably an outlier in the sense that she carried it to such lengths. We were already the top-IQ class in the school, and yet she thought that every gradation in IQ was deeply meaningful.

HB: Well, let's hope she was an outlier. It's amazing you survived.

CD: It is amazing I survived, but at the same time I was fascinated by the concept.

HB: Really? As a young child you were fascinated by it? You weren't traumatized by it?

CD: Well, it's interesting, because I was a winner in that lottery, but the anxiety was tremendous. We all thought to ourselves, *What happens if I take another test and my IQ goes down?*

HB: Right. You have to protect your position at the top of the hierarchy.

CD: Yes. That's how you define yourself.

One day, a new girl came into the class. She had just moved to the school district. And instead of saying to myself, *"Oh, maybe a new friend. Maybe she's nice,"* I thought, *"She'd better not take my seat".*

So, it just gives you this fear. It's a view of the world where you're not wishing other people well: they're your natural rivals and you want your teacher to respect you. So even if you're a winner in that lottery for the moment, it's teaching you the wrong thing.

I also didn't want to go to the city-wide spelling bee because I was already the best speller. Why should I go somewhere else and lose?

HB: Right. You have nowhere to go but down.

CD: Yes. This is a very, very limiting mentality. I knew that I didn't like it at the time, but when that's the main game in town, you play it.

HB: Well, you don't even know presumably. I'm guessing you're not even aware that there's a whole other way of looking at the world.

CD: That's right. At the same time, there was this duality: I had been with these other students for years. I knew they were great students, even if they might have had a slightly "lower number" than some of the other students. It didn't completely make sense to me.

Questions for Discussion:

1. Would you say that you generally have a growth mindset or a fixed mindset? Has your mindset changed in any way as you grew older?

2. Do you know what your IQ is? Has this chapter made you more, or less, inclined to take an IQ test?

II. Confronted by Young Wisdom
Encountering growth-minded 10-year-olds

HB: I'm guessing/hoping that you didn't have Mrs. Wilson-like people throughout your entire academic career.

CD: I didn't have people as extreme as Mrs. Wilson all the way through, but I did carry with me this idea that my claim to fame was being smart, being smarter than many others. So I made sure that I took courses and majored in things where I knew I could do well.

HB: I presume that psychology was one of those subjects.

CD: Psychology interested me; and I thought it was possible—and maybe even easy—to do well. But it isn't easy. It can be a very difficult field. When you look at the other sciences, the problems are agreed upon. The measurement is handed to you, although perhaps you have to do it in a deeper or cleverer way than someone else.

But in psychology you have to take this messy stuff and figure out how to think about it, figure out how to measure it, figure out how to do experiments on it. So in the end, psychology is tremendously difficult, but I didn't appreciate that at the time.

HB: Let's return to your story. You moved through an undergraduate degree and did well. Then you moved on to graduate school. Then what happened?

CD: When I got to graduate school I became fascinated by how people cope with failure. There was research at the time on animals about a phenomenon called "learned helplessness". This research showed that animals who were put in completely unpredictable environments stopped trying to do things: they stopped trying to make things happen because they learned that there was no relationship between what they did and what happened to them.

HB: Since there was no causal link, there was no point in bothering, I suppose.

CD: That's right. And I thought to myself, I wonder if that applies to humans too? I wonder if, in the face of failure, there are people who give up and others who persevere. I would really like to understand that.

Later on, looking back, I wondered, Why was I so concerned with failure? After all, I had never really failed in any appreciable way. But it turns out that when you're in this fixed mindset, failure is always on your mind. Should I take this course? Should I do this task? Should I try this project? What if it doesn't work out? What would that mean about me and my intelligence?

HB: You're subconsciously fixated on failure. The fear of failure motivates everything that you do.

CD: That's right. When you make a mistake, when you say something that isn't perfect, when you don't get something right the first time, what does that mean about you?

And if you have to work hard at something that you think others are doing more readily, what does *that* mean about you? That prospective failure is always there on the periphery of your vision.

HB: But you didn't realize this at the time.

CD: I did not.

HB: How did studying learned helplessness and the potential applicability of that to humans change things? What happened there?

CD: I started with research on children. Something that happened very early on in my research really amazed me: some of these kids were not only able to cope with failure, they seemed to almost relish it.

I deliberately gave them problems that they were incapable of solving—I called them "the failure problems"—and some of them treated these problems very differently. One 10-year-old boy rubbed his hands together, smacked his lips, and said, "*I love a challenge!*" An- other one looked up and said, "*You know, I was hoping this would be informative.*" I thought, What's with these kids?

HB: These were normal 10-year-olds? That doesn't sound very normal to me.

CD: Well, I wouldn't call them normal, exactly: they were very wise, adaptive, and effective 10-year-olds.

Some of them actually ended up solving the problems that they weren't expected to solve because they approached them in such an effective way, using more and more sophisticated strategies that they were teaching themselves on the spot.

On the one hand, I thought they were weird, because it was so foreign from my way of thinking. But on the other hand, I knew that they had a secret, something very wise that they had figured out, and I was determined to understand what that was.

I also wondered if I might be able to somehow bottle that and distribute it more widely, using that knowledge to help myself and other people.

HB: That's what I wanted to ask you. I understand that these kids were different than other kids, but it seems to me that there's a difference between finding unexpected results as a researcher and saying, "*Oh gosh, this actually applies to me. I can somehow learn from these 10-year-old kids.*" Can you isolate any specific epiphany there, or was this a gradual thing that you started realizing?

CD: I think I saw that pretty early in a preliminary way, but the impact of it grew over time, because when you see something so adaptive and you recognize that it's something you don't have, it's something you want.

But I didn't yet understand the full basis of it. So I appreciated it at a distance, but I couldn't fully relate to it yet. I couldn't say, "*Okay, I'm going to do that. I'm going to say, 'I love a challenge.' I'm going to say 'I was hoping it would be informative.'*" I wasn't there yet.

HB: I can imagine that you were wondering, Where did these kids get this from? Are they born with this, or are they being taught this? Is it being reinforced by their parents?

Presumably those sorts of questions spurred on your research.

CD: Yes. In this early research, we found that kids who gave up easily, kids for whom a failed problem seemed like the end of the world, viewed a failure as directly reflecting on their abilities. They'd say things like, "*I'm not smart,*" or "*Oh, I never did have a good memory,*" or "*I'm not good at this.*"

They were interpreting this as meaning something very significant about themselves, whereas the kids who were showing this resilience were interpreting that difficulty or setback as simply meaning that they needed to try harder or try new strategies. One child even said, "*Oh, mistakes are my friends.*"

HB: Really? He actually said that?

CD: Yes. "*Mistakes are my friends. I really learn from them.*" These kids were seeing that they needed to try something different: more effort, new strategies, or what have you.

HB: I can't imagine a kid saying, "*Mistakes are my friends.*" Are these kids who have been specially incubated in the right growth mindset?

CD: Well, over the years I've seen a lot of kids like that. Maybe they were somehow incubated in a growth mindset, but I've seen a lot of them, too many to ignore.

Even very young kids. In some of my work, we say things like, "*Okay, your little doll made a mistake and the teacher was critical of the mistake. What should she do now?*"

And some of them give these whole dissertations to the effect of, "*Well, sometimes it's good when you don't get it right away. Then you can practice and become better at it and the teacher will be happy and you'll learn.*" These are 4-year-olds.

I remember one second-grader earnestly telling a classmate who got a lot wrong on his test what he should do: "*First, try to do the problems. If you can't do it, try two more times. If you still can't, ask someone for help. If you can't do that, do this,*" and so on.

Many of these very young kids have well-worked-out theories about what a setback means and what you should do when it happens.

Question for Discussion:

1. Have you met any "wise children" like Carol describes in this chapter?

III. The Genius Defense

All pain, no gain

HB: When I read *Mindset*, one of the things that puzzled me was why some people cling to some outmoded beliefs in stark contrast to all the evidence that seems to be around them. Let me try to be a bit more specific.

You give a number of examples of people from different walks of life. You talk about what makes an excellent teacher and you highlight that the excellent teachers are those who believe in the growth mindset of all of their students and themselves. They don't regard themselves as these authority figures whose job it is to instill facts in students' heads, but rather appreciate that they're part of the learning process themselves and that their job is to inspire people to improve. They believe that everyone, themselves included, is a work in progress.

Just about everyone I know who is accomplished in any field by any reasonable measure you want to use can point to one or two such teachers that he or she had the good fortune to be taught by. This seems to me to be something that is commonly understood: that there are great teachers, and this is what great teachers do.

Similarly, you talk about great business leaders. You mention people like Jack Welch and other CEOs who are imbued with a growth mindset: they rely upon a team mentality, learning from the people with whom they are working, not looking at themselves as all-knowing authority figures on high.

This, too, I believe, is acknowledged in the social consciousness: that these people have been great CEOs and have done wonderful things.

You talk about athletes, people like Michael Jordan who had to work so incredibly hard to achieve what they've achieved.

So back to my confusion: what puzzles me is that everybody knows all of this. We're confronted almost daily with examples of this sort of thing, and yet it's as if we don't want to pay attention to it.

We seem to want to regard the talented athlete as someone who is just a natural talent, as someone who steps out on the tennis court or baseball diamond and is an immediate hero. We want to believe in the CEO who instinctively knows everything, someone who can just direct everything with a golden touch and never does anything wrong.

So my question—finally—is this: why do you think that, despite all evidence to the contrary, we're so constantly fixated on this golden image of superhuman, intuitive perfection that doesn't actually seem to measure up to reality?

CD: I think that there are a few reasons. First, when you have a fixed mindset, it's very powerful and you see many things through that lens. You focus on what someone has accomplished as a sign of her natural ability. You see Michael Jordan and you think, "*Well, look what he's done. He has to be a form of genius.*"

Secondly, we don't see what people put in to succeed. We don't see their effort. We don't see their obstacles. We don't see their heartbreak. We just see the end product, which makes it easier to assume that, unlike us, they just skated or coasted to this greatness.

I teach a freshman seminar on mindsets every year, and I usually begin by asking students about their heroes. Most of them think their heroes were just born great and that their accomplishments were a natural outgrowth of their greatness.

Then they do research, and it has *never* been the case that their hero did not struggle, did not encounter huge obstacles. Often the hero started out with mediocre talent or was told he wasn't cut out for it. When we see someone at the pinnacle of success and we don't see what she puts in, then we're liable to conclude that she was just born that way.

That's why I like to watch the Olympics. We hear the stories of these athletes' dedication, their setbacks, their resilience. That's what I thrive on.

But I think there's a third reason that we set people up as gods. If we thought that everyone could be special, accomplished, and even great through her own initiative and efforts, then what's *our* excuse?

HB: In other words, it's an easy way out for us to say, *"Well, that person is just a genius."*

CD: That's right: it's an easy way out. *"They just have it. They're geniuses. They're special. That's why they're so successful."*

HB: When the students who are in your class recognize that their heroes are everyday individuals with feet of clay, what reaction do they have?

CD: Well, they've taken my course and they're learning about mindsets, so I think they're generally fascinated. It hooks them in. It makes them think, *"Gee, if I understand more about this process, I can engage in that process more effectively."*

It makes them think about what they want to be in the future and how they're going to get there. It makes them think that it's not about sitting around and waiting to discover what your true talent is, it's about thinking, *Who do I want to be?* and using all the resources at your disposal to get there.

Questions for Discussion:

1. To what extent does this chapter make you want to reexamine what "natural talent" is?

2. How are the concepts in this chapter related to Malcolm Gladwell's book **Outliers: The Story of Success** *and the accompanying notion of requiring at least 10,000 hours to achieve success in a given field?*

IV. Good and Bad Praise
Embracing the process

HB: Another thing that I found very interesting, but somewhat counterintuitive, was when you wrote about praise. While any parent will recognize that he or she should be praising his or her child, you point out that there are two very different types of praise, one good and the other bad.

There is a certain type of praise that reinforces the fixed mindset and another that reinforces a growth mindset.

I'd like you to elaborate on that, but I'd also like to ask you how you stumbled upon that. Were you surprised by that? Because that seems like a very concrete and interesting result that, to some extent, is counterintuitive. I mean, you might say to a parent, *"Praise your child,"* but you wouldn't generally say *"Praise your child in the right way or you might be doing more harm than good."*

CD: I would—well, now I would, anyway.

But to answer your question, it was the mid to late 1990s when we started thinking about praise. I'd been doing the mindset work and we were hearing all these self-esteem gurus tell parents, *"Praise your children lavishly and frequently. Tell them how smart they are. Tell them how talented they are."*

My students and I thought, Well, wait a minute, those kids with a fixed mindset, those vulnerable kids, are *obsessed* with how smart they are and always measuring it. Wouldn't praising intelligence communicate to kids that, first of all, I can look inside you and see this fixed thing; and, secondly, *that's* what I care about, *that's* what's important to me; and therefore, thirdly, you'd better be smart all the time.

It seemed to us that praising intelligence could communicate a fixed mindset with all of its vulnerabilities.

Well, the great thing about research is you don't have to wonder: you can put it to the test. But then we asked, *"What is the other kind, what you might call the 'good kind' of praise?"* We thought about the growth-mindset students and how they were always focused on their effort and strategies. So we thought about *process* praise: praise for the process that the child engages in and the process that leads them towards a good result.

We also understood that this very process was involved in a poor result, but could be improved later. So by giving this process praise, you are not only telling children how to succeed and why they succeeded, you're telling them what to do.

HB: And you're also being unrealistic, as you pointed out in your book, if you praise a child independent of what is really happening. If your kid fails in a competition, and then you tell him, *"You were fantastic. You were really the best one there. The judges were crazy."* Then you're doing a couple of things.

First of all, you're lying, which is generally not good practice if you want people to come to grips with the truth. But in addition, you're not setting up the whole understanding of how much effort is required to conquer obstacles and learn from failure.

You talk a lot about the importance of failure.

CD: Absolutely. We set up studies with different ages of kids, where they worked on a task and then they were praised for their ability or intelligence (the 'bad kind') or they were praised for the process— their effort or their strategies.

And we saw, over and over and over again, that the kids praised for intelligence developed, in that situation, more of a fixed mindset. They didn't want a hard task. When we gave them a hard task, they lost their confidence, their performance plummeted, and they lied about it later.

Because, in that mindset, where intelligence is revered as the be all and end all, they couldn't come to terms with doing poorly, even on something that was new, unfamiliar, and difficult.

But when we praised the process, the effort, or the strategy, they adopted more of a growth mindset about those skills. Most of them—and in some cases over 90% of the kids in a given study—wanted the hard task that they could learn from even if they made mistakes. And when we gave them a hard task later, they stayed confident and resilient and their performance kept improving and improving.

HB: This is what you had alluded to before: the rigorous, scientific research aspect. You have data. You have control groups. You have a way of establishing a growth mindset or a fixed mindset and seeing consequent results in terms of what it is that's been accomplished, together with the associated attitudes.

CD: Yes. And, by the way, many of the kids praised for the process said that the hard problems, the super-hard problems, were their favourites. That praise made them essentially say, "*I love a challenge.*"

Questions for Discussion:

1. Have you ever praised your child "in the bad way"?

2. To what extent do you think that failure is necessary for eventual success?

V. Getting Personal
Popular writing, John McEnroe, and enforcing standards

HB: How has this work been received by your peers in the psychological community? Was there a sense that you had really put your finger on something substantive?

CD: The mindset work and the praise work was generally very well-received in the academic community. We did major research studies with lots of participants. The studies were well designed. The results were consistent. So once we had a body of that work out there, it was quite well-received.
  But I didn't anticipate how difficult it is to get the word out to the broader public.

HB: Is that what motivated you to write the popular book?

CD: Yes. When our praise work came out, it had a lot of press coverage, but it was just a sudden burst of attention within a very short period of time that quickly faded away.

HB: Well, that's why we're doing Ideas Roadshow, Carol—to get beyond this silly trivialization of scholarly work into tiny, forgettable sound bites. We're changing the world.

CD: Good for you. I'm proud to be a part of it.
  Anyway, that's what made me feel that more was needed. Also, my students urged me to write *Mindset*.
  They said, *"We use this. We tell it to our families. We tell it to our friends. They feel helped by this information. They feel their kids are helped by the information."*

I was hearing stories of people trying things they wouldn't have tried. When I taught it in my courses, students would say, "*I had always wanted to do this, but I never had the courage. Now I'm going to do it.*"

An athlete once came up to me during one of my courses. He told me that he was a world-class soccer player but had shattered his ankle and could never play again. He was deeply, profoundly depressed and had no direction in his life.

But the idea that he could develop other abilities—not that he had only this one talent but that he could develop any number of abilities to become something else—gave him hope again.

So, in short, it was largely because my students said to me, "*You've got do it.*"

HB: You mentioned that it was very difficult for you to write the book (and you inserted a parenthetical comment about how, in an earlier fixed-mindset perspective, you wouldn't even be able to admit such a thing). Why was it so difficult? Was it the idea of distilling research issues for the general public without trivializing them, or was it something else?

CD: It was a few things. First of all, academics were not yet writing this kind of book at the time. Everyone's doing it now. But when I started writing *Mindset* very few academics were writing books for the public. That was one thing.

Another thing is that it was very different from academic writing. In my academic writing I always tried to be very simple and clear—and, I hope, at least somewhat interesting. But writing for colleagues in journals is a completely different style of writing. It has no personality.

HB: Deliberately so, presumably.

CD: Yes. But it's not the case that when I'm doing my academic writing all kinds of funny and interesting things occur to me and I have to say to myself, "*No, that doesn't belong here.*" That's not the way it works.

I had to find the appropriate voice for *Mindset*. I don't even know if I would characterize it as a process of learning to write a different way, but I had to learn to access the person I am when I'm with my friends, or when I'm talking to people I don't know: that human person with experiences, hopes, dreams, and funny stories. I had to find a way to access that voice.

HB: I noticed that you made a lot of references to sports. Are you a sports fan?

CD: Yes, I like sports.

HB: You really ripped John McEnroe apart.

CD: I really did. I've been waiting to hear from him.

HB: Well, you really let him have it.

CD: He was such a beautiful example of a fixed mindset, of someone who succeeded abundantly, but nonetheless held himself back, I believe, because of a fixed mindset. In his autobiography he just was spilling out fixed mindset all over the place. I couldn't resist.

HB: I understand. I also would have picked Jeter over A-Rod a little more than you did, but I guess that's a personal thing.

CD: When I wrote the book certain athletes were thriving, and later on other athletes thrived.

HB: Jeter was always thriving.

CD: Jeter was always terrific.

HB: And because of work, I should add, not just because of talent.

CD: Jeter's great. I'm sorry to see that he'll be retiring.

HB: Anyway, you mentioned that academics generally weren't writing popular books at the time. Was there any blowback from the academic community when you wrote yours?

CD: It's interesting. When I wrote the book I thought, Okay, I believe in it. I'm taking this risk. Then suddenly everyone wanted to write a popular book. So it turned out that there was no blowback whatsoever.

But I had to make another decision about the book: whether to put personal things in it. That's something academics absolutely don't do. Yet I felt that if I was talking to people about their mindset, I didn't want to be holier-than-thou. I didn't want to say, "*You have a fixed mindset, but I have a growth mindset. Look how great I am.*"

Instead I wanted to say, "*I've been there. I've struggled with that. I still struggle with it. And struggling with it has given me so many rewards. To struggle to be more in a growth mindset—to be more welcoming of challenges, to be more resilient in the face of setbacks, just this impetus to go for it, to go do things that are risky and that you might not have done before—that has brought so many rewards to my life.*"

I wanted to tell that story, so I did.

HB: Did some people misinterpret it? I could imagine that there might be some people out there who would be very, shall we say, "old school", trumpeting their belief in standards, associating this book—unknowingly, unthinkingly, and doubtless unread—with a type of touchy-feely attitude that somehow deviates from real accomplishment and standards.

It's very clear from everything that we've said before that nothing could be further from the truth: that in fact, what you're talking about is a way of developing *higher* standards, of achieving *greater* things, of becoming a *more* knowledgeable and capable person. But still: were there people who said, "*This is just some new-age silliness*"?

CD: I really made sure to emphasize throughout the book that adopting a growth mindset isn't lowering standards, that adopting a growth mindset is about setting rigorous standards that you can attain over time through dedication.

In our research, we always look at grades and test scores, not because we think that scores are the be-all and end-all, but because we're showing over and over again that those grades and test scores are a natural byproduct of engaging deeply and effectively in a learning process that the growth mindset promotes.

You'll meet those rigorous standards more effectively with a growth mindset. We've shown that teaching a growth mindset to students raises their grades, makes them stay in school longer, and so forth. A growth mindset inspires you to set and reach the most rigorous standards in an effective way.

Questions for Discussion:

*1. Do you think that the personal touches Carol adds in **Mindset** played a contributing role to the book's success?*

*2. Are there times when academics **shouldn't** write popular books about their research? If so, when might that be?*

VI. Brainsets

Neuroplasticity and intelligence

HB: Another thing that I enjoy about your approach is that you bring into play important aspects of neuroscience and cognitive science in quite a natural way.

By explicitly telling students and teachers about how the brain functions, about the plasticity of the brain, about how the brain learns, you're doing two things simultaneously, it seems to me: you're informing people about brain functionality while simultaneously promoting a growth mindset by showing what contemporary science is saying about the learning process. You're highlighting the fact that contemporary research is suggesting that it's not all innate, that it's not all about what's in your genes, while underscoring that our very knowledge about how we learn is also changing, also evolving.

Have you had partnerships with people in the cognitive science community who say, "*This is interesting. I'd like to study mindsets from the perspective of functional MRI. I'd like to look at what's going on in the brain when people are thinking in one way or the other?*" Has there been any of that?

CD: Yes, absolutely. I've engaged in some collaborations, while other researchers have also looked at this sort of thing. For example, Jason Moser and his colleagues at Michigan State University recorded the electrical activity from relevant parts of the brain as students with a fixed mindset or a growth mindset worked on a task and made errors.

HB: What did they find?

CD: When students with a growth mindset make an error, the relevant parts of the brain light up orangey-red, which shows heightened activity indicating that they detected the error, they're processing it deeply, and they're correcting it.

When you look at the same parts of the brain when students in a fixed mindset make an error, you see almost nothing. Green, cool, cold. They detect the error and they flee from it as quickly as possible.

HB: I spoke with Stephen Kosslyn recently. As you may know, he's written a popular book called *Top Brain, Bottom Brain*, which summarizes research he and his colleagues have done regarding different areas of the brain. The basic idea seems to be that the top part of the brain, the frontal lobe and parietal lobe, are more involved in planning and processing information and that a comprehensive theory of personality would need to take that into account somehow.

I would imagine that people who are in the growth mindset, who are thinking and adopting those challenges and trying to find a solution and thus actively engaged in plotting and planning and scheming, would have more activity in those parts of the brain when faced with challenging problems.

CD: Yes. But it depends on what you're plotting and planning and scheming.

HB: Sure. They could be plotting to run away.

CD: Right. And thinking about how you're going to cope with a given setback. We've shown in our work that people in a fixed mindset will find all kinds of strategies for repairing themselves after a setback. They'll compare themselves to people who did worse, rather than finding out how to do better, for example.

HB: Or, as you said, they'll lie.

CD: They'll lie. They'll go over and over easy problems so they'll feel good at it, rather than tackle the harder ones.

I'm really excited about the explosion of research speaking to the plasticity of the brain. For example, a study came out a few years ago that followed a group of teenagers across a period of four years, showing that there were large changes in IQ for some of the kids that were parallelled by changes in the density of neurons, nerve-endings, in the relevant parts of the brain.

This idea is that, if you use it, you'll grow it: your connections will be strengthened and the density will be increased. It is very exciting. It puts kids in charge of their brains and it tells them that what they're doing now makes a difference for them.

HB: And it's scientifically rigorous. It's our best understanding of what's actually going on.

CD: Yes. It's not saying everyone is the same, or anyone can be anyone or anything, but it's saying that you can really grow your brain through hard work, good instruction, and so forth.

I'm also very excited by work in cognitive science that's identifying the components of intelligence, of "executive function," and figuring out how to teach it.

Intelligence has always been this mysterious thing that some people seem to have and some don't, and that Mrs. Wilson thought was embodied in these little scores. But now there's a growing recognition that it's a set of skills, many of which can be taught or enhanced, which is really exciting.

Questions for Discussion:

1. In this chapter both Howard and Carol refer to aspects of the brain's "executive function" capacity. What is that, exactly?

2. Before reading this book would you have been willing to accept the claim that "intelligence is a set of skills"?

VII. Gender Differences
Male and female mindsets

HB: As you were talking, it seems that one sport that strikes me as the paradigmatic fixed-mindset sort of activity is golf. So many of these guys—sorry, but they're mostly men, at least the ones that I know—begin every round thinking that they're Tiger Woods.

They have this image of themselves as possessing some completely unrealistic level of ability, and any contradictory data that they receive—which typically occurs after the first swing or two—will be disregarded, or somehow interpreted as an exceptional happening. They will lie. They will cheat.

Most don't look at themselves as a golfing work in progress, and the score of the day is everything. All told, it strikes me as pretty close to the apex of fixed-mindedness.

CD: Yes. And some of that comes from being in a competitive situation where they think, *Well, I can't be a loser, because that will make someone else the winner.*

HB: Yes. And just a moment ago, in an off-handed comment, I mentioned that—regarding golf at least—this seems to mostly apply to men. But more broadly, is there any sort of gender differential happening here? Can you make any generalizations, in terms of culture or expectations, that—in our society, at least—men are more (or less) prone to adopt this fixed mindset mentality than women? Or is there no correlation whatsoever with mindset and gender?

CD: Well, there's no general, overall, consistent finding that males or females have more of a fixed or growth mindset.

But when females have a fixed mindset, it hurts them more. Men, when they have a fixed mindset, are more likely to think, *It's fixed, and I have what it takes,* and it's hard to shake that in them.

Females, on the whole, tend to have less of that overwhelming confidence, so a fixed mindset combined with low confidence, or shaky confidence, is a real liability: *My ability is fixed, and I might not have what it takes...*

The other thing is that, in many fields, women might encounter negative stereotypes. In STEM fields, in certain humanities, like philosophy, or in certain social sciences, like economics, there are often negative stereotypes about women. In the corporate world there are also negative stereotypes.

A negative stereotype is a fixed-mindset judgment: it's fixed, and your group doesn't have what it takes. When a female already has a fixed mindset, it's hard to withstand that stereotype, especially in these areas where there are many other challenges, struggles, and setbacks.

So if you're in a fixed mindset and you are struggling, you might think, Well, maybe they're right.

But if you have a growth mindset—we've been showing this in a number of studies with females in computer science and math—you're able to withstand these stereotypes or setbacks better because you think, *This is a learned set of skills. Maybe my group wasn't highly represented or didn't do as well traditionally because of those stereotypes, because those fields had fixed views about us, but it's a learned set of skills and I'm going to do it.*

Questions for Discussion:

1. Based on Carol's comments in this chapter, what impact do you think female role models would have on other women who suffer from a fixed-mindset perspective?

2. Why do you think that, on average, men have more confidence than women? Is this purely due to sociological factors, genetic factors, or a mixture of the two?

VIII. Getting the Message Out
Inspiration and misinterpretation

HB: How do we get your message out? If we want to enhance and improve our educational system there has to be a way of exposing teachers to your findings in the best way possible. There has to be a way of making it scalable. You can only give so many talks yourself. So how do we go about doing that? How do we take these ideas that you and your colleagues have developed and tangibly implement them in schools and in the public milieu for the benefit of all?

CD: We're working very hard. Last May, the White House had a conference on mindsets.

HB: How's Obama's mindset, by the way? Does he have a growth mindset?

CD: That's not up for discussion. Anyway, I was very pleased that the White House recently held a conference on growth mindsets and how to scale our interventions.

What came out of that conference was a research network that is now launching a national study that will bring our mindset intervention to schools across the country, and we'll be able to evaluate which groups it works best for, what settings best foster growth mindsets and enhance the effectiveness of our intervention, and how we can make it work better for all different groups.

We're very excited to be taking our growth mindset workshops to a national level.

We're also launching a whole line of research on teacher practice. We're rigorously evaluating different kinds of practice and we're also asking, *"What are ways in which teachers may misinterpret our findings?"* We're finding a lot of teachers are taking the praise work and saying, *"Well, you just have to tell kids to try hard."*

HB: Really? That's a gross misinterpretation. How can they possibly conclude that?

CD: Well, because praising effort seemed to do some good in certain circumstances and they assume that means you should just universally tell kids to try hard. And nine times out of ten when a teacher or parent says, *"It's not working,"* I ask them:

> *"Are you telling your kid to try hard?"*
> *"Yeah"* they say, *"Isn't that what I'm supposed to do?"*
> *"No,"* I reply, *"That's called nagging."*

We've shown in a very large-scale study that telling kids to try hard or, *"If at first you don't succeed, try again,"* has no impact because kids in a fixed mindset hate effort: they think if you're smart you shouldn't need it.

So that often winds up just being insulting. And just telling a child to work hard when he doesn't know what to do or how to work effectively, is not going to work. That runs the risk of having someone simply conclude that she's not good at something.

But instead, we're finding that if you tell kids, *"Remember, when you work hard at these problems, you grow your math brain,"* or *"Remember, when you do hard problems, you become better at math,"* that **does** have positive results. Kids are very motivated by this connected idea that, *When you do this or that, you grow your brain.*

HB: And as we talked about earlier, I would imagine that teaching kids about the many others who have accomplished so much after having encountered many failures, difficulties and obstacles can also have a very positive effect.

CD: Yes. But only when the child or individual understands the growth mindset. Just telling them, *"This person worked hard to succeed,"* is not enough, because they might think, *"But I shouldn't have to do that if I'm good at it."*

They may not believe Michael Jordan worked very hard; they may think he just worked a little bit, but that was just on top of his natural talent.

HB: It wasn't integral to the whole process.

CD: That's right—they might conclude that he was an exception.

A growth mindset, then, creates a context in which you can fully understand that that hard work is growing your brain, growing your talent.

Questions for Discussion:

1. How would you describe to a friend or colleague the difference between "trying hard" and "adopting a growth mindset"?

2. What role can federal governments and central authorities play in helping to ensure that teachers are aware of the importance of growth mindsets?

IX. Practical Tips

Beneficial struggling and the power of "yet"

HB: If I'm a teacher in Sacramento, say, and I'm thinking, *This is interesting. How do I learn more about this? How can I expose my colleagues to this knowledge?* What, concretely, can I do about this?

CD: First, I would read my book *Mindset*. I'm also affiliated with a company, mindsetworks.com, which has a teacher toolkit and a school toolkit that helps schools start implementing growth mindsets at the different levels. Many schools and school districts have now declared themselves growth-mindset schools.

One thing that people have found effective is to start with a group book-read and discussion, one chapter per week. Another thing that people have found effective is recognizing that everybody is a mixture of the mindsets.

If you say, "*Growth mindset is good, fixed mindset is bad,*" everyone will say, "*I have a growth mindset,*" whether they actually do or don't. They'll deny fixed-mindset thoughts. They'll disown them. But they won't change them.

So I think it's important in group discussions to say, "*Look, we all have fixed-mindset thoughts at one time or another. We all think,* **'I could never do this', or 'This student will never learn this', or, 'I know the smart students from the not smart ones', or, 'It's the school's job to figure out who can learn and who can't'.**

So many whacky, fixed-mindset thoughts are going through people's minds all the time. It's important to own them and examine them as we change to move toward a growth mindset.

It's also important to legitimize why teachers might have had a fixed mindset. They may have had their own version of Mrs. Wilson.

It's important to say, *"We used to think this, but now neuroscience is leading us to think that, and it's exciting to explore the implications for how we learn and how we teach."*

Many teachers are used to being the authority, rather than thinking of themselves as fellow travellers with their students, who are also growing their brains. Many teachers in growth-mindset schools are now saying to their students, *"Thank you for helping me grow my brain,"* or they might say to a student, *"When I understand how you're struggling, it helps me be a better teacher. Thank you for helping me grow my brain."*

HB: You do realize that Mrs. Wilson will go down in infamy, right?

CD: Well, I hope she leaves a very positive legacy. I'm grateful, because her teaching has inadvertently led us to these insights that are helping people. How can I regret that?

I'd like to tell you about a few more things that we tell teachers. We tell them to talk about struggle, to make it a good word—who's having a fabulous struggle?

I actually worked with a department in a big Silicon Valley company, and now they're talking struggle. They existed within a culture of genius, where it was not acceptable to be wrong, or make a mistake, or not look like you have the highest IQ in the world. That was very restrictive. Apparently they're now being so much more creative and innovative since they're talking about what they're struggling with. It's not a shameful thing. They're embracing it.

Teachers should be talking about struggle too, telling students that that's when they're growing their brains the most, that's when their neurons are really making these stronger connections. Struggle, struggle, struggle.

We're also doing research on an incredible word, the word "yet". I learned of a high school in Chicago where students had to pass 84 units to graduate, and if they didn't master a unit they got the grade "not yet".

I thought, How fantastic! The students were going around asking, "*How many 'not yets' do you have?*" They'd never do that if they got a failing grade.

"Not yet" means that there's a learning curve, and you're not at the end of it, but you're *somewhere* along it. Just hear the difference if a child says, "*I'm not good at math **yet**. I can't do it **yet**. I tried, but it didn't work, **yet**.*"

It's doing a few things. It's putting them on a learning curve. It's telling them that you have the expectation that they can succeed through their efforts and your instruction. It's a fantastic word that turns a fixed-mindset statement by the child into a growth-mindset idea.

HB: All of these ideas strike me as not only important, but also as quite concrete. You're not just talking about abstract concepts here: you're highlighting particular techniques that can be used, that can be directly implemented.

Is this something that is being embraced by teacher education and teacher training?

CD: I think that teacher training is absolutely essential. We haven't made a push to infiltrate teacher-training programs yet. But my impression is that more and more of them are incorporating these ideas because they are research-based. They're concrete. And they are easily implementable.

I'm hoping that over time we will develop more and more materials that can inform educators exactly how to implement these ideas and techniques.

Someone came to me recently representing a country, saying, "*Our schools are failing miserably. How can we use the growth mindset across these schools, many of which are in poverty?*"

I hope one day to be able to hand them something and say, "*Here. Take this.*"

Questions for Discussion:

1. Should more schools implement a grading structure that incorporates a "not yet" as a mark?

2. Is rote learning compatible with cultivating a growth mindset?

X. Diversity and Universality

French, Americans and common ground

HB: Much of what we've been discussing so far seems most directly relevant to the United States, but, of course, we're talking more generally about people's self-belief, confidence, motivations, self-defense mechanisms, and all the rest of that. We're discussing basic issues of the human condition.

But I can also imagine, as you try to move forwards and have impact in different parts of the world, that you might potentially run into other cultural issues, other ways that people transmit information, other values regarding what should or shouldn't be sometimes admitted or accepted.

You have an anecdote in your book about how you were in Provence for some time and, while you enjoyed it, you couldn't help feeling this sense throughout that you were involved in taking some sort of a test. Then one day you had lunch in Italy and you felt suffused with feelings of acceptance and warmth because of the different cultural environment.

I've spent quite a bit of time in France, and not only do I have some personal appreciation of what you mean by this notion of feeling that you are regularly taking a test, but I've also developed a sense of awareness that, to a large extent, the entire country also feels that way. That's to say, the people who actually live there and who were born there often feel the same way. It is, I think, an essential aspect of the French culture.

CD: Some people said I should take that out of the book, but I didn't.

HB: Really? Why?

CD: Because it was a national stereotype.

HB: But…it's true. So I'm glad you left it in.

Not all people and all cultures and all societies are the same. We all know that. Which means, I'm thinking, that different programs and different attitudes and different solutions will work differently in different places.

CD: Yes. We are tremendously interested in cultural differences. There are many cultural differences even within the United States.

Stephanie Fryberg, a wonderful researcher at the University of Michigan, grew up on a Native American reservation near Seattle. She went back and transformed the elementary school there in terms of growth mindsets, and the results were amazing. The kindergarten and first grade moved from the bottom of the district to near the top in a year and a half.

I bring this up because, at first, when she introduced the idea of growing your brain, there were some positive results, but then when she took into account cultural values and explicitly introduced the idea of growing your brain so you can one day help your family and contribute to your community, the results were suddenly overwhelming.

We always have to be aware that we're plugging into a value system, and give reasons for why kids might want to grow their brains. That's just one example, but I think it represents the kinds of challenges we might meet in different parts of the world.

We've started to look at data from South American countries, European countries, Asian countries, and it does look like mindset, or something like mindset, is playing a role in achievement across the board.

But, if we want to go in and have an impact, we absolutely have to learn much more about the values and practices of those particular cultures.

HB: And there's also the factor of the way that other cultures might look at your work, and American tendencies in general. We talked just now about the French and the sense of feeling like you were always in the middle of taking some sort of test, and what effect that has.

But my sense of what it's like to look at America from the French perspective (and perhaps the English too) is that there's often this sense that, *"Oh, these Americans, they're always going on about the importance of confidence, but the problem with many of them is that they have too much confidence. Far too many of them walk around thinking that they know everything, when, in fact, they are often quite ignorant."*

So I'm imagining that you might be forced to say, *"Hang on, these are not issues that are unique to America."*

CD: That's right. These are fundamental ways of seeing the world that seem to be more or less universal. And it isn't about confidence, in fact. As it happens, the people who are strutting around thinking they know everything are actually those who have a fixed mindset.

In a growth mindset, you're not puffing up people's confidence, you're telling them that they can develop themselves to accomplish something later. It's about rolling up your sleeves and doing it, it's not about talking the talk.

And what you were saying before is actually true: international research shows that our students are among the most confident in the world, while not being among the highest achievers.

So the right answer is clearly not to merely inflate people with confidence, but instead get kids to use the appropriate strategies to put in the effort and develop the motivation that they need to accomplish things.

Questions for Discussion:

1. Do you think that some countries or regions would be naturally better (or worse) at promoting a growth mindset than others? If so, which ones and why?

2. Why do you think that Americans appear to be, on average, more self-confident than other nationalities?

XI. New Horizons

From school bullying to Middle East politics

HB: What sorts of things are you most excited about doing in the future?

CD: We've been applying our mindset research to a variety of other issues. With my former student David Yeager we've been looking at how mindsets play a role in bullying and aggression in high schools. He's been designing very effective interventions to combat aggression, using a mindset framework.

We also have a whole program of research on peace in the Middle East.

HB: Really? That's ambitious.

CD: We have research showing that when you teach Palestinians or Israelis a growth mindset, their attitudes towards each other improve and they become willing to entertain serious, major compromises for the sake of peace.

HB: Are these children that you're talking about?

CD: No, these are adults. Some of our participants were members of Fatah and Hamas living in the West Bank. When you have a fixed mindset, you say to yourself, "*Those people are evil, deceptive, duplicitous, violent, and will never change.*" There's no basis for compromise or trust. But if instead you think, "*People have the potential for change. They are a certain way now because of the environment, because of the political situation, because of their leaders and what they may be* *fomenting, but everyone has the potential for change"*, then you create a real opportunity for meaningful change.

We have a big project where we're designing more major workshops that we hope will create the growth mindset and help it last over long periods of time.

HB: How do you do that? How do you go and engage with these people?

CD: We have an incredible collaborator, Eran Halperin at the Interdisciplinary Center in Herzliya, Israel, who works with a number of different organizations to do this research.

HB: I'm guessing, without knowing anything about this, that you might be preaching to the choir a little bit, that the very people who are willing to sign up for these sorts of programs are already those who are sufficiently open-minded and either already have, or are willing to adopt, a growth mindset.

CD: In our initial research, we found that the biggest impact was on the most radical or right-wing people.

HB: Really? How do you get them to participate?

CD: The original research was done by a survey company, and we worked our interventions or experiments into the material. But now we're developing these broader workshops, and they're in the context of leadership workshops.

Questions for Discussion:

1. Do you think that there's a link between having a growth mindset and the ability to empathize with others?

2. Is it easier to adopt a growth mindset as a child than as an adult? Harder?

XII. The Big Picture
Growing the human condition

HB: Looking at psychology as a whole, where do you see the field going? Aside altogether from your work, where do you see the cutting-edge areas being? What advice would you give to some ambitious, capable, growth-mindset young person who's thinking of moving into this particular field?

CD: I think psychology is more exciting now than it's ever been.

When I went into psychology, personality psychology was about putting people in boxes: *are you this kind of person or that kind of person?* At the time, most of psychology was not relevant to anything people cared about. But now that has changed completely. The most eminent researchers are doing things that matter to the world, matter politically, matter in terms of well-being, matter in terms of longevity.

The other thing that's so exciting is that I believe we're changing our view of human nature from something very static to something that's capable of tremendous growth.

This is not just in my work: psychologists around the world are developing interventions that are looking to change very basic qualities, looking to change people's situations and their behaviour quite dramatically. This whole idea that we can grow into people who are more productive, more effective, and more caring, is just so exciting.

HB: That's tremendously inspiring. Are there any dark clouds on the horizon? Are there any things that worry you?

CD: There are always dark clouds. You're always going to have critics. There are always going to be naysayers, and you may also have people whose science isn't as sound as it should be.

But I think that in the end this trend towards making a difference is so important, and the things that really work will last.

HB: That's great. Anything that you'd like to add?

CD: I don't think so. I think we've covered a lot of ground.

HB: I think so too. Well, thank you very much Carol. I've really enjoyed this.

CD: It's been a pleasure.

Questions for Discussion:

1. Is psychology more scientific today than it was 30 years ago?

2. Are there any downsides to professional psychology being more relevant to everyday life now than ever before?

Continuing the Conversation

Readers are encouraged to read Carol's book, *Mindset*, which goes into considerable additional detail about many of the issues discussed here.

The Mind-Body Problem

A conversation with Janko Tipsarevic

Introduction

Giving Your All

It's hardly a secret that the sporting world is awash in tedious, knee-jerk clichés: *We're just taking it one game at a time. We'll get 'em next time. It's time to step up.* For my part, nothing drives me running screaming from the TV faster than hearing about that infamous "110%"—*This time it will be 110%. I knew I had to give it 110%. We're here today because every one of us gave it 110%.*—a truly inane combination of the hackneyed and the nonsensical.

But lurking in this mathematically illiterate hyperbole lies the nugget of something actually very meaningful: *how much time and effort does anyone—even a phenomenally talented person—need to spend on something to achieve genuine excellence?* How many other personal interests have to be sacrificed along the way? How much single-minded focus is required to be the best?

Janko Tipsarevic is a worthy case study. After a glittering junior tennis career, he spent years of his early professional life mired in the mid-level rankings before suddenly breaking out and establishing himself at the very highest echelons of the sport, spending the better part of two years firmly ensconced in the world's top 10. And this at a time that is universally recognized as nothing less than the golden era of men's professional tennis: a fearsomely difficult task.

So what happened? How did this almost miraculous transformation occur?

Well, by his own admission, Janko, has sometimes had a hard time focusing exclusively on tennis. He loves to snowboard. He loves to DJ. And he also loves to read.

As it happens, the fact that he has occasionally evinced an interest in 19th-century German philosophy and has a Dostoyevsky quotation tattooed on his left arm has, rather predictably, led to him being publicly anointed as a "tennis intellectual", whatever that means—it's hard enough to understand, after all, what a "non-tennis intellectual" is.

But the interesting question is not how it is possible that a professional athlete could conceivably make his way through an entire book by Friedrich Nietzsche, but whether or not doing so would have any real effect—positive or negative—on his active life.

Well, you might think, it's just a book. But a hallmark of great literature is that it is provocative, driving one to reflect, to question prior beliefs and assumptions. A good book, in short, leads one to doubt.

Which is, for the most part, a very good thing. "*Doubt is not a pleasant condition,*" Voltaire wrote, "*but certainty is absurd*". Bertrand Russell, with characteristic irony, put it slightly differently: "*The trouble with the world is that the stupid are cocksure and the intelligent are full of doubt*".

Doubt, then, is the inevitable ally of healthy scepticism, a necessary antidote to being led astray by our own egos and unjustified sense of infallibility. Most of us could do with a good deal more of it.

But then, most of us are not professional athletes, where unwavering confidence in one's own abilities and on-court possibilities—"objectively justified" or not—is nothing less than integral to success.

For someone like Janko, the tension was inevitable.

> "*It could be that some of these books were even influencing me in a bad way, because all these big minds, these philosophers, are seeking the truth. And most of them, at the end of the road, they find depression, hate, and so forth: something that is not really positive.*
>
> "*If you are surrounded every day by these thoughts of, 'Why? Why? Why?', then you start to question a lot of stuff in your life and, of*

> *course, on court: 'Why is this tournament going to change my life? Is this important? Is this real happiness?'*
>
> *"And tennis is not about that."*

But unhelpful literary stimulation was hardly the only issue, or even the principal one. Achieving real excellence, he came to appreciate, meant that he had to do much more than simply give his all when he was on the court. He had to rearrange his life off the court as well.

> *"I wanted everything. I wanted to try everything and do all sorts of stuff. Maybe I had this thinking or feeling or urge that life is too short and I really wanted to experience it to the fullest. But this was one of the things that was setting me back.*
>
> *"I was finding all sorts of stupid things and maybe even excuses to get upset about, to spend energy on; and then when the tennis match came I knew that I hadn't given 100%, which meant that, psychologically, I was less disappointed if I lost.*
>
> *I'd say to myself, '**Sure, if I would do these things differently I could play better, but who cares?**' It's like an alibi that you have in your mind which makes you deal a little bit better with a loss."*

In other words, Janko was suffering from a classic case of a limiting fixed mindset, unwilling to genuinely embrace the challenge of testing how good he could be for fear of failing, and in the process severely limiting his chances of achieving his true potential.

So what happened? How did Janko eventually unchain himself and adopt a growth mindset?

According to Janko, the turning point was very easy to pinpoint: it came through the intense experience of shared, single-minded dedication with his teammates that culminated in Serbia's successful Davis Cup campaign.

> *"I felt so much joy and so much happiness when we won—it was the best moment of my professional career. And I remember thinking to myself, at the age of 25 or 26, Time is flying: I'm not a kid anymore."*

And suddenly, Janko was en route to a spot in the world's elite top 10. It hardly happened overnight, but from that point forwards, he would simply not be denied.

Well, you might say, he had it coming to him—after all, he is supremely talented. But to hear Janko himself tell it, that's not the right way to look at the situation.

> *"Talent definitely exists, but I believe much more in the hard work that you need to put in to arrive at this point. It's more like the 10,000 hours that Malcolm Gladwell talks about in his book, Outliers: it's not just work on the court but off the court as well.*
>
> *"Maybe from the outside it looks like we're leading a boring life, but as I said, if you don't give 100% of your attention to tennis, it's really hard to use your maximum potential.*
>
> *"In my experience, when you lose, the first emotion that you feel is disappointment because you lost a match. If you gave everything you could before and during the match, the disappointment slowly fades away. But if you didn't, and you were acting stupidly and doing something that you shouldn't do, in my experience, the disappointment slowly turns into anger. Then you get angry with yourself and you are angry with people around you and they don't understand why.*
>
> *"And I know that when I stop playing tennis and hang my racket on the wall and say I'm done, I will have this huge regret that I will need to live with for the rest of my life if I didn't do my best.*
>
> *"It's OK to fail. But it's not OK not to try."*

Just another sporting cliché? Well, consider this.

> *"Look, I'm in a phenomenal situation. But it means that the aspect of this business that is just flat-out hard work is very important to me—it's the one thing that I feel is really in my control. If I didn't do that I would kick myself forever."*

Those are the words of renowned particle physicist Nima Arkani-Hamed, explaining why he chooses to focus his time on research rather than actively pursue his other interests.

The problem exists everywhere and there's no need to reach for oxymoronic phrases to describe it: honestly giving 100% is hard enough.

The Conversation

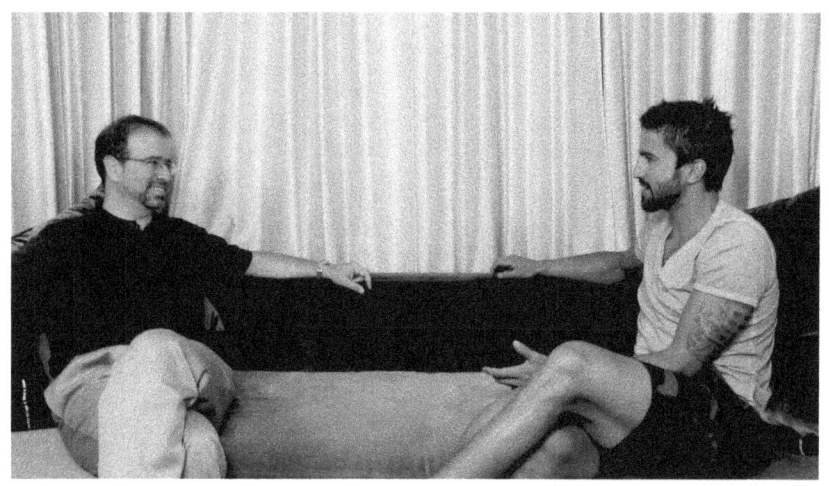

I. On Nietzsche and Tennis
The dangers of too much perspective

HB: On your website, you list three people you'd like to have coffee with: Friedrich Nietzsche, Salvador Dali and Al Pacino.

JT: I need to update that. I would still probably talk with Nietzsche because he is my favourite author and I've read a lot of his books. I don't agree with him completely—in fact, there's a lot of stuff I don't agree with—but I love the way he writes using this nihilistic approach to life where he puts everything to ground zero and starts building up a theory from there, independent of the current human society or the place and time we are living in. Since there are so many influences on us at any given time, I think we just forget what and why a particular thing is really important.

So that's one person for sure.

HB: What would you ask him?

JT: I honestly don't know, because I think whatever he wanted to say he wrote in his books. I would probably be overwhelmed talking to a guy who's been dead for a couple of hundred years, but I guess I would ask him just, "*Why? Why do you think like this?*"

I would just try to go deeper into the subject. I haven't read any of his books in the last two or three years, which I probably should have, but I would probably just be really overwhelmed having a dead, smart guy sitting next to me.

HB: Well, even a dead, stupid guy would be a bit overwhelming.

JT: Exactly. I would love to have a coffee with Al Pacino. He is my favourite actor and a guy I'm still hoping to meet one day. I'm a big fan of his movies, together with all my family back home. And as for number 3—I don't really know why Dali is there. I saw a painting of his once that I liked, but I'm not really a big art guy.

HB: Well, we can forget about him. He's dead too.

You just mentioned that you don't get a chance to read that often. My sense, knowing very little except for when I was a kid playing junior tennis, is that it must be very difficult for you to be reading these sorts of works when you're on tour. How does that work?

JT: I'm not ashamed to admit that when I was reading these kinds of books I wasn't ready. I was too young. I was trying to read Dostoyevsky when I was 15 or 16 and I can see now that I wasn't ready to read them.

In fact, it could be that some of them were even influencing me in a bad way, because all these big minds, these philosophers, are seeking the truth. And most of them, at the end of the road, they find depression, hate, and so forth—something that is not really positive.

If you are surrounded every day by these thoughts of "*Why? Why? Why?*", then you start to question a lot of stuff in your life and, of course, on court—"*Why is this tournament going to change my life? Is this important? Is this real happiness?*"

And tennis is not about that.

HB: That's exactly what I wanted to ask you, because in my mind this is all about doubt. It's about self-doubt, it's about questioning yourself.

JT: Exactly. I got this love of literature from my mom. She finished law school but she decided to stay home with the kids. She was reading a lot of books, so I also read a lot of books. But maybe it was too early to read some of the deeper stuff because it really didn't influence my tennis in a good way.

HB: Do you have a conscious sense of this? Do you say to yourself: *"Well, I shouldn't be reading this now. I'll put it aside: I've got a tournament coming. The last thing I need is to have my head filled with doubt or questioning"*?

JT: Exactly. I'm not saying that I'm not reading those books at all, but it's tough to digest. I love the feeling of a movie or a book that leaves an impression on me, of not having a need to read another book for the next month or so because the last book was so powerful that I still question it, agree with it, disagree with it. It's a great feeling. But sometimes, as I said, it's hard to digest.

HB: Is there a positive aspect to this? Let me speculate for a moment. Suppose I'm a professional tennis player and because I have this interest in literature, I can imagine that it might help me, perhaps after a tough loss, because it might give me some kind of perspective. I might say: *"Well, I understand certain aspects of the human condition, I have a bigger picture. I've read about all these horrible things that have happened to people and I have a broader perspective than a typical professional tennis player who might live in a cosseted bubble. So I won't get too down after a tough loss."* Is there any sense of it helping in some way?

JT: I wouldn't say that it was helping in terms of becoming a better tennis player in any way, but I have a feeling that I may be a better person because of it. Maybe I have some deeper understanding of some things than other people who didn't try to read and engage with some of these authors. But these are all, as you say, just speculations. I don't know.

I should stress here that I don't want to say that I'm smarter or I'm better than anyone else. Maybe this has given me a broader perspective on life. But what I can *definitely* say is that Nietzsche didn't really help me feel better about myself when I lost a tough tennis match. That's a straightforward answer that I can give.

Questions for Discussion:

1. Under what circumstances is the possession of broad, diverse interests counterproductive to success?

2. Is there a type of literature that one can be "too young" to read? Should young people be actively discouraged from reading certain works until they reach a certain age?

II. Lost Opportunities

Reflections on vacuous press conferences

HB: One of the things that frustrates me is that when people say, "*I enjoy literature—I like Nietzsche or Schopenhauer*", it comes across in some circles as being pretentious. And that frustrates me because it implies that anybody who wants to read any of these books is simply doing it for show—they're not actually interested in the actual content. Do you find that happens to you at all?

JT: I do. Quite a lot. And I'm really trying to run away from it a little bit. I am quite open to speak to you about it now because I see that your whole show is about honestly trying to find a connection, but it's really frustrating for me when I'm in a press conference and I get hit by these questions of, say: forehand, backhand, serves, schedule and then somebody just throws in a question about a Dostoyevsky tattoo or whatever.

I even stopped answering them, just saying: "*Please don't ask me those questions, because it makes me look like I'm trying to be smart, or whatever. This is just a hobby that I like doing.*" I agree that there are not many tennis players on tour who like doing it but it's simply a hobby that I personally enjoy. I'm not trying to be pretentious or smug, it's just that I liked reading some of these books.

Some of them I didn't like. It's also nice when you read a book and you say, "*I don't agree. This is not true.*" This also helps you to have a broader perspective towards life. At least that's how I see it.

HB: Right. Well, it's interesting that you mentioned press conferences. As an observer, as somebody who watches tennis, I may see the occasional press conference, but I generally try very hard to avoid them because more often than not the questions strike me as just completely inane. If I were a tennis player, I'm sure I would get awfully tired of having to respond to the same types of questions: "*How did you feel after you won?*" or, "*How did you feel after you lost?*" There's nothing really substantial that seems to be going on, and I can imagine that's fairly frustrating on your side.

It seems to me almost designed to highlight this image of the "dumb jock". This is one of the reasons I wanted to talk to you. You're obviously a thoughtful guy. You're obviously someone who cares about all sorts of different things. You care about life, you have some perspective, and you're a professional tennis player all at the same time. Does it frustrate you, this constant, stereotypical focus on these sorts of questions?

JT: Yes.

HB: You can do better than that.

JT: I'm kidding. It's just that you had a five-minute question…

HB: Yeah, I know. This is why I'm a crappy interviewer too, you see. I'm probably no better than those lousy journalists, actually—except I'm not a journalist.

JT: I'm just joking. But seriously, if there is something to say, I really feel the need to say it. Obviously if you lose a match 6-2, 6-0 there's nothing to say: you just had a bad day. For a disappointing loss or an easy win there's not much to say.

But if there's more to the story, perhaps I try to share a little bit more than the other guys. I try to say how I was feeling, what I think I could have done differently or better, really going deeply into the game, into the tactics and my state of mind during the important moments.

But on the other hand, the media is sometimes pretty hard on us. You really need to be careful with what you say, because if you happen to choose some words that are not exactly spot-on then sometimes they make a much bigger deal about it and write about it in a way that you didn't really mean.

HB: I don't want to put you on the spot, but just to satisfy my curiosity: do you get the sense that the people who are asking these questions really understand the game? You're clearly someone who can reflect on the game and talk about interesting psychological points, interesting aspects of the turning points and so forth. But it seems like those sorts of questions rarely get asked. That's what I mean about often feeling frustrated as a tennis fan.

JT: To be honest with you, it really depends on the tournament. I have to say that many journalists, especially in the Grand Slams, really know their thing. They come prepared, they do their research and most of them ask the questions which need to be asked so you can open up. Sometimes if you're not asked the right questions you don't really have anything to say.

But, of course, there are some events and tournaments where, say, tennis is a new sport and they're coming in a little bit unprepared and most of the questions are, "*How are you feeling?*" or "*How was your serve?*" I mean, there's nothing wrong with that—it's just that in some other countries tennis is not yet in the culture of the people and therefore the journalists do not have any real idea of what they need to ask the players to make an interesting interview.

HB: Well, I appreciate your tolerance. But for me, on the receiving end, there *is* something wrong with this, because I think, *Here's this guy on the screen in front of me and I want to get some information*. You just played this match and I want to know more than just that you felt good when you won or bad when you lost, which I'm pretty sure I can guess before the interview starts.

JT: Well, I think that is one of the things that separates the good journalists from the bad ones. I'm happy that you want to know more about me and that you want to ask the right questions. But sometimes some of the journalists, as we say, just come to work from 9 to 5: they come because they need to be there, they ask these questions that they feel need to be asked and then that's the end of their work day. They're not really challenging themselves or the guy who needs to answer their questions.

Questions for Discussion:

1. To what extent is the image we have of athletes shaped by the media?

2. Do you think that post-match interviews with athletes are better, worse, or just the same as they always were? What sorts of questions would you like to see athletes asked that they rarely are?

III. Commitment

More than just the hours

HB: Let me ask more about your particular interests off court. You have lots of hobbies, not all of them literary or cultural, although some are. Is this unusual compared to other professional tennis players, you think?

JT: I think it is a little bit unusual, and this was one of the things that was setting me back. I wanted everything. I wanted to try everything and do all sorts of stuff. Maybe I had this thinking or urge that life is too short and I really want to experience it to the fullest.

You know, the life of a tennis player is not easy. If you don't give tennis 100% of your time, life and attention, you have no way in hell of using your full potential. When you give everything and you fail it's much better than when you don't give everything and you fail, because then, deep down inside, you know that you could have done better. This has nothing to do with forehands or backhands on the court.

One of the reasons that I broke through into the top 100 was because I was always a hard worker on court. I had a Russian coach for 13 years who disciplined me and made me practice really, really hard, but the difference was that outside of the court I wanted to try skateboarding, snowboarding, roller skating, going to discos, dying my hair, doing piercings all over my body, doing tattoos. All these things take away bits and parts of your energy and attention that you could be using for tennis.

HB: How does it work now? Now that you're not doing all that, what are you doing instead?

JT: I still have hobbies. My biggest hobby is music by far. I still love DJing, the only problem is that the different time zones don't really add up. I do sometimes go out, but maybe twice a year or something like that. Now I just devote my attention towards tennis 100%. I'm 29 and I'm hoping that I'm going to play until I'm 30-something, and that's only a few more years.

The good thing is that the more you're in it, the more you enjoy yourself. If you start looking at this lifestyle as a prison, you're going to start to resent the very thing that you're trying to become: a big tennis player.

But at the end of the day, the more attention to detail I put in—whether it's to fitness, nutrition, stretching, recovery or practice—the more I enjoy it. I'm really loving my life right now.

HB: I imagine you'll go to a bookstore or to an art gallery or be DJing or whatever, and think to yourself, *Gosh, I'd like to know more about this* or *I'd like to do this thing more often*. But then you say to yourself: "*No, no, I'll wait till later. This is my time to really be focused on tennis. This is my time to realize my full potential*". Is it that kind of compartmentalization?

JT: It depends on what kind of hobby it is. My biggest passion, by far, outside of tennis is snowboarding. I started skiing when I was 2½ years old and I've skied and snowboarded all over Serbia and Europe. But for the last four years it's been on hold: it's just too dangerous because of tennis.

I love DJing in nightclubs but that is also on hold, or I'm not doing it as often as before, because I need to get up early the next day. It's always OK to read a book—but you need to do everything in moderation, because everything you do too much outside of tennis takes away and consumes energy.

Maybe from the outside it looks like we're leading a boring life, but as I said, if you don't give 100% of your attention to tennis, it's really hard to use your maximum potential.

HB: This is completely on par with other conversations I've had. I mean, I've talked to theoretical physicists, for example, and they'll say exactly the same sort of thing: *"If I don't give 100% to doing physics right now, I'm not going to be able to have that breakthrough."* This is not unusual.

JT: No it's not. The only point is that my thinking before was that even if I went out and got drunk the night before I would still show up the next morning at 7 am on the court and practice.

HB: Well that *is* different: a physicist wouldn't do that—show up at 7 am, that is.

JT: Well, I'm taking the extreme example. I would still practice and work hard and then I would do double damage to my body. I would feel bad that I did a bad thing and instead of recovering I would then practice.

When I talk about giving 100% during this crucial period of my life right now, it's not just in the moments when I'm on the court. I'm not saying: *"OK, let's eat a plate of Buffalo chicken wings, a pizza and a cheesecake and hope that tomorrow morning I will feel better."* Because if I were to do that, I would indeed practice the next day and I would give 100% on the court. But it's not going to be the same Janko as the guy who did something different the night before.

Questions for Discussion:

1. To what extent is a focused dedication to excellence learned behaviour? Might there also be innate dispositions or tendencies to regularly invoking a high level of commitment to one's development?

2. What role does honest self-assessment play in the world of top-flight international competition? In what ways is it as important for the achievement of success in other less competitive activities?

IV. Breaking Through
Leaving nothing back

HB: One of the things that has amused me and to some extent confused me is this idea of a 'role model'. You get these guys who are marvellously successful athletes or actors or whatever, and even if some are incredibly selfish or superficial, all of a sudden there's this sense that they should be an example for the youth of today on how to live a proper moral life or something.

JT: But how would you define a role model? What is the definition of a role model for you?

HB: That's a good question. I'm not sure I even believe in role models. Maybe that's my problem.

JT: When I was a kid, I always liked Andre Agassi because of how he played tennis. I honestly never cared about what he was doing off the court, his personal life or whatever. It's the same with me for actors and movies. Personally, I experience, say, Al Pacino, through his movies. The rest is not very important to me.

All these top guys, not just in tennis but in every other sport, have this devotion to being the best. But what I feel they all have in common is that they hate losing. They really, really, hate losing. Some of them are not good losers; and even though others will say, *"The other guy was better than me"*, deep down they're thinking, *I'll get you next time.*

I don't think that there is such a thing as a role model which has every aspect covered.

To be a top tennis player you need to be selfish. You need to have a bigger ego because you're alone. It's not easy: you don't have a teammate to pass the ball to. It's really amazing to see the records that some of the players in this era now have—I mean, how bad does their bad day have to be to lose?

I follow soccer and I love Barcelona. You have these times where Messi or Iniesta is not performing well but somehow the team wins because there are eleven of them. But in these individual sports where you have superstars that have been so dominant over the last 3, 4, 5, 10 years, it's amazing how good they are, all alone, all this time.

You can have the support of your coach, trainer, wife, fitness coach, but at the end of the day when you step on Centre Court you are completely and absolutely alone.

HB: Why do you think that there is so much consistency now in the very top players?

JT: If you ask me, my answer would be that the surfaces are much more similar to one another than they were 10 or 15 years ago. Obviously I'm not undermining champions such as Rafa or Novak or Roger, but the surfaces are now very, very similar. So players who are on top don't have to go out of their way and change the way they play in order to win Slams or big events.

Rafa Nadal doesn't need to play serve and volley to win Wimbledon. If you look back a few years ago, you had players like Goran Ivanisevic, Pete Sampras and Richard Krajicek who were all serve and volleyers. Nowadays, do you really see the difference between David Ferrer's play on clay or on hardcourt? No, it's exactly the same. He still has time enough to run around his backhand and the surface is still fast or slow enough to allow him to do the same thing, with minor changes, on each and every surface. And this is what is creating superstars, in my opinion.

HB: So it's the relative constancy or relative similarity of the surfaces that allows for such high consistency of the players?

JT: Exactly. Also I have a feeling that it has a lot to do with the balls. I think—I'm not sure—that they've made the balls a little bit bigger. They don't fly as fast as before. It wasn't all that fun paying 200 pounds to come and watch a Wimbledon match where you watch Pete Sampras just serve aces. It just wasn't fun.

HB: It was fun for him, probably.

JT: Well, yes, probably for him. And it was easier on his knees.

I mean, tennis has evolved so much, and technology as well. If you look at the rackets players were using, say, even seven or eight years ago compared to now—or the strings, it's a huge difference. It's much more of a power game now because, in my opinion, the surfaces for most of the events have become so slow that you really need a lot of power to put the ball back.

In my opinion, if this stays the same, if they don't change the surfaces, the future of tennis will be this transition—which the top two guys right now are the best at—from defense into offense.

Because the surface is slow enough, combined with the technology of a faster racket and faster strings, you now have the chance in one or two shots to come back from, say, four metres behind the baseline to one metre inside, waiting for the short ball on the forehand.

HB: And because the surfaces are slower, not only do you have this transition from defense to offense, but you also have incredibly long points and incredibly long matches. I mean, it's just getting longer and longer and longer. It seems to be unusual to have a Grand Slam tournament these days where you don't have quarterfinal or semi-final matches of five hours or something. It just seems like a remarkably heavy toll on your bodies. Is this sustainable at all?

JT: It's not easy. As I said, more powerful rackets and more powerful strings are helping, and also this constant work on yourself. When I say "yourself", I mean technique: *How can I do the most damage while spending the least amount of energy?* Because to win a Slam you need to win 7 best of 5 set matches. And some of them can be in blistering heat, really hot weather; New York can get so hot and humid. Melbourne, at the Australian Open, can also get ridiculously hot. Obviously you have to have the right tools—the racket and the strings—but it has a lot to do with technique.

If you look at the top guys now, they are always improving their technique, how they play. Roger Federer is not the same player now as he was six or seven years ago; he's playing differently. He's using more and different parts of his body to spend less energy but he's still doing the same—or even more—amounts of damage.

HB: When you talk about using less energy, that brings up another point I've often wondered about. Suppose you're playing a match in a slam and you're up two sets to love, and it's a blistering, hot day, and you go down a break or maybe two breaks in the third set. Is there a sense, psychologically, where you say to yourself: *OK, I'm just going to conserve energy and not push myself as hard in order to conserve my energy?* Or does that not factor into the equation? How does that work?

JT: Well, maybe some players are doing that, but most tennis players don't. In my mind, all of us think the same thing, *You need to fight for the next point. If you fight for the next point it's going to be OK. Just don't worry about it.*

All of us have entourages—some bigger, some smaller—who are travelling with us and making sure that we are fit and ready. But in the end, how many more US Opens are you going to play? Two? Three? Four? That is, if you're not injured. You cannot afford not to fight for every point. In my mind, this is the healthy approach. If it's hot for you, it's hot for the other guy—and in this case the other guy is two sets to love down.

Maybe some of the other guys do it but I would rather try, especially when I'm not injured and when I know that I'm fit enough, I would just prefer to fight for every point and see what's going to happen.

HB: Let me go back to the point you made about the surfaces, how they're quite similar and therefore the style of play is similar, which allows for such consistency of the top guys. Are there other people talking about this? Is there talk among tour players or people who run the ATP of maybe going back to the days of distinguishing the surfaces a little bit more, or are you an outlier here?

JT: I honestly don't know. I mean, tennis has never been more popular—we've created so many superstars in the last couple of years. Don't get me wrong: the top guys are there because they're good. And there still is, I tell you, in terms of moving and sliding and playing, a big difference between grass and clay, and all these top, top guys have won tournaments on every single surface in the world: indoors, outdoors, hardcourt, clay court, whatever. But I don't think or feel that there is going to be a change coming soon.

I mean, look at when Pete Sampras was playing. He was the #1 player in the world for so many weeks, but still when it came to clay or some other such event he struggled. Or think of all the Spanish players who were dominating the European clay court season but when the indoor swing started they were not playing so great. Now you don't really have that.

HB: Or even before that. I mean, it was a huge deal that Borg could win so many titles at Roland Garros and win at Wimbledon as well—those were considered two polar extremes. And there were always these guys from Latin America who'd do really well at Roland Garros and then get killed in the first round at Wimbledon. But now, as you say, it's completely different. I've certainly noticed that all these top guys are always there. All you have to do is look at the semi-finals of the Grand Slams. It's just incredible. It's remarkable.

JT: It really is amazing. But they have one big thing in common: they live very simple lives. Their only devotion is to be the #1 player in the world or to win this Grand Slam or whatever. And this is the only thing they really, really care about.

I am much, much better in the last two or three years and this is one of the reasons why I broke into the top 10 and have played London for two years straight. Before, I was thinking that some of the things in my life are more important than they actually need to be.

The only important thing—apart from the health of your family and friends and everything—is tennis. And you should be very angry with yourself if you didn't do something that you could've done to be a better tennis player. I was finding all sorts of stupid things and maybe even excuses to get upset about, to spend energy on; and then when the tennis match came I knew that I hadn't given 100%, which meant that, psychologically, I was less disappointed if I lost.

HB: You had a back door.

JT: Yes, you had a sort of alibi. And I know a lot of very, very good juniors who had the same problem.

I was the #1 player in the world under 14, 16 and 18—and I was playing under 18 at 16½. So I was incredibly talented, but I was also just stupid and crazy in my head. And when I started playing the pros I was doing some other stuff on the side, and then when I had a disappointment I wasn't *really* disappointed because I said to myself—

HB: You had left something back.

JT: Yes. I'd say to myself, *Sure, if I would do these things differently I could play better but who cares?* It's like an alibi that you have in your mind which makes you deal a little bit better with a loss.

HB: So what changed for you?

JT: The big turnaround was winning the Davis Cup in 2010.

HB: That's when you guys shaved your heads, right?

JT: We shaved our heads, yes.

HB: Is that what did it? Shaving your head?

JT: Well, no: we made that deal at the beginning. I mean, we knew in principle that we could do it. I think that Novak was ranked #3 and I was somewhere in the top 30. We also had Viktor Troicki who was around 34th and Nenad Zimonjic who was the #1 player in the world in doubles. So we had a very good team, we knew it was possible. We saw the schedule: we only had one away game in Croatia and everything else we played at home. But we never thought that we could actually win it.

HB: Really?

JT: You see, a lot of things need to come together for a country to win the Davis Cup for the first time. There were other countries like Spain or France or the United States who had done it something like 15 times before. Not many countries have won the Davis Cup, maybe only 13 or 14 different countries. Serbia has 7 million people, which is less than New York City. We obviously believed that we had the skills to do it, but to win it actually would be such a big deal because Serbia had only been a member of the World Group for a couple of years. Just being part of the World Group was actually amazing.

And I remember I felt so much joy and so much happiness when we won—it was the best moment of my professional career. And I remember thinking to myself, at the age of 25 or 26, *Time is flying: I'm not a kid anymore.*

HB: You are, by the way. You are still a kid.

JT: Well, OK. But in tennis years I'm not, I promise you. And I thought to myself, *I really want to make the most of my career*. Because I knew that when I stopped playing tennis and hung my racket on the wall and said I'm done, I would have this huge regret that I would need to live with for the rest of my life if I didn't really do my best.

It's OK to fail. But it's not OK not to try.

In my experience, when you lose, the first emotion that you feel is disappointment because you lost a match. If you gave everything you could before and during the match, the disappointment slowly fades away.

But if you didn't, and you were acting stupidly and doing something that you shouldn't do, then in my experience the disappointment slowly turns into anger—you get angry with yourself and angry with the people around you and they don't understand why.

But it didn't come immediately—it's actually an interesting story. The first tournament of the year, in India, I was in the semifinals and was in a set where I was something like 4-0 up, and I lost the match. And I was really, really devoted; I had psycho-eyes. I was into it 100%. I swear to you, I was never like this before. And I lost. I called my brother and I said to him, *"Doesn't matter:* **this** *is my year. This year I will be in the top 20 and I will win my first ATP title."*

Next tournament: Australian Open. I play Verdasco, a top 10 guy; having 5 match points and an overhead in the middle of the court and whatever, and I lost. Again, I remember I was in a room eating cheeseburgers, being completely depressed, and I called my brother and said, *"It doesn't matter: this will be my year. I can feel it."*

Next tournament: I fly to Johannesburg—a 7 million-hour trip, and I lose to a wildcard, 7-6, 6-7, 7-6 with match points and whatever and **again** I remember that I called home and I said, *"It doesn't matter: this will still be my year."*

HB: Your brother is still taking your calls at this point?

JT: Well, he was probably a bit sceptical. But my point is that I was really trying, I was really pushing. I don't know one person who tried and did it immediately from the first go. But if you try, and if you really give 100%, in most occasions it will happen for you.

Questions for Discussion:

1. Have you ever invoked the type of "alibi" that Janko mentions here? How common is doing so?

2. To what extent can Janko's change in attitude after Serbia's 2010 Davis Cup victory be viewed as the adoption of a growth mindset? (Readers interested in the particulars of growth mindsets are referred to the Ideas Roadshow conversation, **Mindsets: Growing Your Brain** *with Stanford University psychologist Carol Dweck.)*

V. Tennis as a Team Sport
Davis Cup and doubles

HB: Let's talk a little bit more about Davis Cup, because you mentioned just now that that was the highlight of your career. You talked before about how you're alone when you step out onto the court—it's just you, you're all by yourself and you have to deal with it. But of course, Davis Cup isn't like that, Davis Cup is a different feeling. Were you always passionate about the Davis Cup?

JT: The Davis Cup is my favourite competition in the whole year, and we also won twice in an event called the World Team Cup in Dusseldorf, where 8 nations competed with each other. I have a feeling that I was born to play a team sport, because I really feel like a team player. This upcoming Davis Cup will be my 14th year in a row. There are a couple of guys on tour who've played more matches than me and more years consecutively—maybe Lleyton Hewitt—but not too many, I promise you.

The main reason why I play—obviously I love my country and all that patriotic stuff—but the main reason why I play is because I like my teammates so much. If this week were a struggle for me, if I was thinking: *Oh my God, I have to spend a week with these guys I don't like* or whatever, I would never have had the kind of run that I've had.

This is so much fun. I have so much energy during the event, I feel like a teenager. The three of us have dinner and then go into a room and just talk about anything. It's something that you don't have on tour. Generally, you finish your match, finish your practice, you stretch with your physiotherapist and you go to your room to watch a movie and recover and that's it. These Davis Cup weeks are really, really special.

HB: Is there a sense that you *have* to do that normally: that you have to put up that barrier while on tour? I mean, if we talk about someone like Novak, presumably you see him all the time—

JT: I don't think you have to do it, but it just saves energy. If we're all in the same tournament we'll go out for dinner at least once per tournament, but it's not like we're locked up in a room until the next practice or match. It's not the same energy, it's not the same feeling.

You might play the other guy before the draw is out or whatever. During a Slam especially everybody is much more focused on what's going on in his own little circle. But in the Davis Cup, it's not like that. This is one of the reasons why I enjoy playing it so much. And we have a solid chance of winning it again this year.

HB: I wanted to talk a bit about nationalism in tennis. You've talked about how the Davis Cup is such a positive experience for you—feeling like a kid again and being with teammates and so forth—but there is this aspect of nationalism that comes into play.

You mention that tennis has never been as popular as it is now, and I don't know the statistics but I get the feeling that tennis is not as popular in the United States as it probably should be, given the quality of the players and the quality of the matches.

My sense is that the reason for that is because there just aren't any Americans anymore in the top 10 so there isn't any nationalistic identification. Do you think that's true or am I completely off base?

JT: Well, the point is that, just to give it to you straight, Sampras and Agassi and all the American champions who have come before spoiled the United States of America in terms of looking at tennis players.

HB: But, I mean, Why should I care? I like to watch you play and I'm not Serbian. I like to watch Federer play and I'm not Swiss.

JT: Well, it's because you're a tennis fan. But there are simply a lot of people who are not tennis fans. There used to be a point where someone would just turn on the TV, in the golden era of American tennis, and they don't care about tennis but if they see Agassi they're going to leave the TV on and watch Agassi play.

I have a feeling that if we don't have any big champions in Serbia in the following years it's really going to be tough on the new players that are coming through.

In the last four years, our country of 7 million people had 4 different #1s. Ana Ivanovic was #1, Jelena Jankovic was #1, Nenad Zimonjic was #1 and Novak Djokovic was #1. I was #8. Viktor Troicki was #12.

So imagine in, say, ten years when none of us are playing anymore and somebody comes in at #15 or #18—which is incredibly tough; it's really tough, I'm telling you—people will just say, *"What's up? What's going on?"*

My coach is German and he told me that a similar thing happened in Germany after Graf, Becker and Stich. Some new players came who were still top 10 but they were effectively ignored.

Now look at the Americans. John Isner is a great player, but I think I heard the other day that for the first time in I don't know how many years the USA didn't have a top 20 male tennis player, which is not good for tennis in America.

HB: So Serbia, this tiny country of 7 million, how does that even happen? How do you guys manage to produce so many great players?

JT: There is no real explanation. Serbia as a country had a lot of political difficulties in the last fifteen years: a lot of wars, a lot of bad politicians leading our country. But it was all individual hard work and help from our parents. I'm not blaming the Serbian Tennis Federation or whatever, it's just that in these tough times tennis was the last thing on people's minds.

HB: Is there a sense that there is more of a hunger when people are going through difficult times?

JT: In one way there is. I still believe that if you are a born champion it doesn't really matter how rich your parents are or how much money you have when you're young. But in one way it is true that you will have more hunger for success when you come from these tough and difficult times. This was one of the reasons why so many Russian female players were so good, say, five or six years ago. I think at one point they had six Russian women in the top 10. It was really amazing.

But in Serbia, it came from nothing. And now the Serbian Tennis Federation is doing a little better with the programs and the kids and everything, but it's still far, far away from what it needs to be, considering the success that Serbian tennis players have brought.

HB: A few minutes ago you mentioned Zimonjic. Do you believe that doubles players, as a general rule, get the respect they should? To take one example I know you're very familiar with, there is this Canadian guy, Daniel Nestor—born in Belgrade, as it happens—who has won all these Grand Slams and all these matches...

JT: More than 900 matches.

HB: Right. And I don't have a sense that someone like that is actually given his due. Is that your sense?

JT: I think it is, especially now. When I was starting on the ATP tour I really had a feeling that these doubles guys were not doing anything. I never saw them do fitness. I didn't see them do stretching. It was just serve and gliding to the net—you know, doing ballet.

But now—and I'm telling you this from what I see going on—all these guys are working almost as hard as the singles players. I really do feel as if they deserve much more credit than they're getting at this moment.

HB: If you go to a tournament, it's clear that the fans really enjoy doubles. But they rarely seem to be broadcast on TV.

JT: They need to put them more on the main courts to give them more exposure. That's one thing.

And sometimes it might seem a bit too fast: serve and volley, serve and volley, serve and volley. Especially on grass.

I'm guessing that as a spectator it's fun to see this 30-shot rally that ends with a guy who makes a passing shot from the fence and then everybody rises to a standing ovation or whatever. You don't see that sort of thing very often in doubles because the basic dynamic is a big serve and a good volley from the guy who is at the net, and that's not really the Hollywood version of spectacular.

Questions for Discussion:

1. In what ways does the presence of a teammate affect the psychological state of an athlete? Are some athletes more "naturally disposed" to team sports than individual sports?

2. Are you affected by the nationality of an athlete? Should you be? What, if anything, does this say about our need to strongly identify with specific social groups?

3. To what extent can nationalistic competitions, such as the Olympics, be regarded as positive ways to "channel" innate human tribal tendencies?

VI. Achieving Potential
Coaching and talent

HB: Let me ask you some more specific questions about sports psychology. You talked about giving your all and the change that's happened to you. Do you prepare for a match differently now compared with before? Is there a sense of being mentally tougher somehow then you were before?

JT: First of all, I became mentally tougher by working much more outside of the tennis court. If you are fitter, physically, you are able to be tougher, mentally, because the mind and the body, as you know, are connected.

If you are physically fragile and you get tired very fast, no matter how much determination you have you will not be able to be mentally tough. So the first step is that you need to be really, really fit.

The second step, what helped me, is this attitude that we just talked about a few moments ago: fighting for every point. Don't look at the scoreboard, don't think about what's going on, don't speculate on how you might save energy or how you might try to shorten up the point or whatever. You need to be fit enough to know that you're able to fight for every point.

Just keep it really, really simple. I know it's a cliché and you've probably heard it a thousand times but in my case it really *is* like this: the less I speculate, the easier it is for me. But the first step is that you need to be fit and ready for it.

HB: You must have thought about coaching. I know you've done some mentoring through your work with Tecnifibre—I've seen some of the videos—and clearly you have a very penetrating and lucid way of being able to look at the game. You're a thoughtful guy and I'm sure other people have pointed this out to you—that you would make a very good coach later on in your career when you're an old guy like me. Is that something that has ever crossed your mind?

JT: I will hopefully play tennis for a couple more years. At this point I can say with certainty that I don't see myself as a full-time travelling coach, but I'm pretty sure that I will be connected to tennis in one way or another. We opened up a tennis academy in Belgrade recently and it's working great. Together with my coach, manager and a couple of other associates we also opened up a managing agency and we signed up quite a few players. I'm also doing the Tecnifibre Next Generation program, which is helping to tutor young guys and give them a taste of life on the ATP World Tour.

HB: And you seem to really enjoy that—it comes across.

JT: I really do enjoy that a lot because a good coach can make a real difference. It helps that I played. It really helps that I have experience, so I know how a player will feel in certain kinds of stressful situations on and off the court. I have a great coach who helped me so much and taught me so much.

I believe that at one point, I might take up what I'll call a "project": if I see the hunger, the will and the potential in someone who can be the world #1, I have the feeling that I would take the challenge.

I hope that I won't ever have to coach just for the money but instead will be in the position where I can be enthusiastic about the idea of taking somebody and help bring them to the very top.

HB: When people talk about talent, at some point that seems to almost lose meaning at your level. Everyone seems to be able to hit every shot and do so many things so well. If you take yourself out of the equation, do you say that the guys who are #2 in the world or #3 in the world are really much more talented than the people who are, say, #15 or #20? Or is there something else that's going on? Is it will, focus, dedication or fitness? Is there a way that you can say, "*No, this guy is just way more talented*"?

JT: I believe that talent exists but I believe much more in the hard work that you need to put in to arrive at this point. It's more like the 10,000 hours that Malcolm Gladwell talks about in his book *Outliers*: it's not just work on the court but off the court as well. It includes watching YouTube videos—*How is this guy moving his feet?*—this is also the work and research which you need to do.

You shouldn't, as a professional, wait for your coach to spoon feed you the information, *you* need to be the guy who goes out looking for that information. It's more like *work, work, research, work*; and then at one point it will click and you will say, "*Oh, there it is*". And when you get it, then you start working on it and processing it.

I still believe that the guys at the top are working more, and are more professional, than the guys who are not at the top. I believe in talent also—you can say that some players are more talented than other ones—but I'm a much bigger believer in finding the route to success to be at the top.

HB: So, natural talent is not the dominant factor in this.

JT: No. I know quite a lot of junior players who played with me who were actually better than me and were incredibly talented. They had such a great touch and could do amazing things with the ball, but they never broke through because they didn't accept the hard work that comes in between to put that talent into actual play.

HB: Could you give me an example of something that your coach will say to you that you won't notice yourself, or perhaps something you did notice but didn't fully appreciate? What are the sort of things a professional coach at your level would say? How would he help you?

JT: A good coach, in my experience, will tell you stuff when you need to hear it. It's not about pointing out mistakes—that doesn't really help. It really depends on the situation.

For example, today we had an hour practice on one of the courts and I played horribly and I didn't really try in the best possible way. I was staying too far back or whatever. Then we had a 15-minute gap between one court and the other and we sat and talked and he told me, "*We have 45 more minutes. I know you're feeling lousy and it's hot and humid. It's not your day. But just do this, this and this. Just focus on these three things. Focus on your ball toss on your first serve, focus on moving your feet right after you hit the shot—because my feet were just horrible today—and stay down on the return, don't go up with your body. Don't think about anything else.*"

I believe in simplicity in terms of coaching because if you feed your player too much information then he starts over-thinking and not focusing on the right things. A coach should point out one, two or three things max that should be focused on and just let the player find his own way. Because, as I said, at the end of the day you are completely alone on the court. The coach's job is just to push you in the right direction so you find the highway.

HB: To me, as a spectator, I look at the level of anticipation the top players have, how soon they're able to pick up the ball off their opponent's racket, and it just seems crazy-good and much better than the level it was 20 or 30 years ago.

When I look at the top players and the way they move, their range in terms of being able to turn from defense to offense and how they're able to do that, it seems that the only way they're able to do that is being able to anticipate so much faster than they were used to. Am I off base here, you think?

JT: Honestly I don't know how it was 20 or 30 years ago. For most or almost all of the top guys, the general idea is that you have this boss attitude on court: *I am here and I will play my game. I will try to make you dance as I play.*

When you try to play your game, you anticipate much better because if *you're* the guy who is trying to push the other guy around it's much easier to see where the ball is going, rather than being too defensive. We say, *Are you acting or reacting?* If you're acting and you say to yourself, *OK, I'm going to do this, this and this*, it's much easier to anticipate. But if you're reacting to what the other guy is doing, then you're suffering much more because you're always on the back foot and you're being pushed around on the court.

Nobody has ever played great tennis just by being defensive. Defense is a big part of tennis right now because, as I said, surfaces are much slower than before, but nobody was ever a top 10 player only by being defensive.

Questions for Discussion:

1. Do you think Janko would make a good coach? What do you think would be his strengths and weaknesses?

*2. Does **anyone** have the potential to be a top athlete if she puts the hours in? On average, which requirement for international sporting success do you suppose is harder to attain: the necessary physical skills or the correct psychological approach?*

VIII. Winner Take All?

Spreading the wealth—or not

HB: You mentioned the players' entourages earlier, and I'd like to talk a bit about that.

If you're a top 5 player, you've got all sorts of money, you've been winning all sorts of tournaments, you have all sorts of sponsorship deals, so you can hire a physiotherapist, a psychologist, a nutritionist; you can travel with ten different people who are explicitly there to help you.

But if I'm #150 in the world, I can't do that. I simply don't have the financial resources to be able to do that.

In your view, does that give some sort of systemic advantage, financially, to the people on top to stay on top because they have the resources necessary to be able to hire all these people to support them?

JT: With respect to this, I don't see that it's unfair because most of us had to go through it.

HB: Sure. But I didn't say it was necessarily unfair.

JT: OK. But my point is that what *is*, let's say, sometimes less than completely fair, is that some countries or federations have funds to help their own players—they might provide them with a coach and a fitness trainer from their national federation's budget. And it's a great thing. If Serbia had the funds and the resources, I know that they would do the same for me. But they just don't. They help as much as they can.

I agree with you that in tennis the top players are earning a substantial amount of money, but if you go outside of, say, the top 100 it's a struggle, I have to say.

And it's very unfair because tennis is one of the top five sports in the world in terms of popularity, so to be in the top 150 in the world and be forced to struggle to have enough funds to buy your coach a ticket and pay him a salary and feed him everyday, it's a bit unfair I have to say.

HB: Let's talk about the ATP. Is there anything that needs to be changed in professional tennis?

JT: So you're really trying to get me in trouble now...

Well, Grand Slams increased the prize money, which is great because they're aware, as I told you, that tennis has never been more popular—not just men's tennis but also women's tennis. In the last few years we have had so many more champions, and this is a good thing.

And I'm not talking about the top guys—because the top guys have their endorsement deals and whatever—I'm talking about what we just spoke about: the guy who is #150 and who doesn't have enough funds for his coach, his wife, and so forth.

So that's better, that's a step in the right direction. It's a constant fight. Slowly, step by step, it is getting better. The only difference is that players are the ones who need to take the initiative.

HB: If memory serves, Andy Roddick was taking an increasingly vocal role about structural issues shortly before he retired. I don't know if that's directly related to what you're saying now, but your primary concern seems to be ensuring that those who are much lower down in the rankings get a bigger slice of the pie.

JT: Exactly. And it has improved. I mean, I'm really not following this—I had a chance to be on the Council but I decided not to because it takes away a lot of energy and time. But the recent increase in prize money mainly benefitted the lower-ranked players because most of the money was pumped into the first four rounds of a Grand Slam, which was good. But I still think that we need to focus more on making sure that the players who are ranked #150 or #200 or whatever are benefitting more from playing professional tennis.

HB: I understand that you're worried about being taken out of context and all that, but what's wrong with using the media and saying exactly what you're saying to me now: *"Look, there really is an asymmetry which is not healthy for the sport and we have to balance things a little bit. These guys who are #150 in the world are phenomenal tennis players who, because of the structure of the system, sometimes really can't make ends meet, and if we don't address this we risk shortchanging our future."*

JT: I don't think that people want to hear that. They don't really care if the guy ranked #150 has enough to pay his coach.

HB: So there's this sense that they are all just spoiled athletes.

JT: Yes. I mean, I'm not crying here for help or whatever, but I'm just saying that the general media and population, I can promise you, really don't care if the guy who is playing the qualies at the US Open and is ranked #150 has enough funds to support his coach to come here with him. I swear to you they do not care.

HB: I'm sure you're right, but objectively it's better for the game, right? So if you're a tennis fan, it's important to realize that something should be done.

JT: This is why I say it is a step in the right direction. I just feel that it could be a little bit better.

HB: Fair enough. Is there anything else I haven't asked? You've given me an awful lot of your time so I don't want to keep you.

JT: I'm really good. I cannot believe 1½ hours has gone by already.

HB: I've got to let you go back and rest and win this thing (*this conversation occurred right before the start of the 2013 US Open*). I know you want to win it for yourself, of course, but think of what it'll do for **me**—focus, man.

JT: That's additional motivation, for sure.

HB: Thanks a lot, Janko.

JT: Thank you very much.

Questions for Discussion:

1. *Do you agree with Janko that nobody cares about the issue of ensuring that lower-ranked players have sufficient resources to continue competing in professional tennis? If so, what does this say about our sense of fairness in the sporting realm? To what extent is it different from other realms?*

2. *Has this conversation given you unique insights into the world of a top athlete? To what extent has it impacted any prior beliefs you might have had about the life of professional sports?*

The Science of Emotions

A conversation with Barbara Fredrickson

Introduction
Only Connect

Why do we smile, laugh and actively seek out personal connections with the people around us?

This might seem like the sort of particularly obtuse question that only a pointy-headed scientist would ask. We do it because we want to, of course, because it makes us feel good—why else?

Well, yes, comes the steadied scientific reply, but why does it feel good? What evolutionary purpose do our so-called positive emotions serve?

After all, from an evolutionary perspective, negative emotions are fairly straightforward to understand: we feel fear, anxiety or distress, and the accompanying physiological responses enable us to avoid enemies or predators and adrenalin surges through our veins, our senses become much more acute.

But love? Feeling all warm and fuzzy inside? Telling a joke? What's the point of that, evolutionarily speaking?

Barbara Fredrickson was one of the first people to extensively grapple with this issue head-on—surprisingly enough, it wasn't that long ago before those pointy-headed scientists got around to asking the question in the first place.

> *"As the science of emotions began to develop, there was kind of a 'cookie cutter' template used for all emotions:* **Emotions promote specific action tendencies that had helped our ancestors survive threats to life and limb.**

> *"And if you use that for understanding the evolutionary value of emotions, it's easy to just leave the positive emotions out. There were theories of emotion that were saying, "**This is how emotions evolved**", that didn't even **mention** positive emotions, which I find pretty amusing, given their obvious existence.*
>
> *"What I did in my early work is to point out that we can't use the same theoretical framework to understand the value of positive emotions. In particular, the timescale is different. The adaptive value of a negative emotion is during the moment of threat, preparing you to do some action that is evolutionarily advantageous. But with positive emotions, there's no clear action tendency that's going to save your skin right at that moment, because, most often, there is no threat."*

For Barbara, positive emotions are nature's way of training us for future challenges. Rather than the knee-jerk survival responses that negative emotions provoke, positive emotions provide a key mechanism for enabling us to develop innovative ways of dealing with complex, unforeseen scenarios in the much distant future. The fact that positive emotions make us feel good naturally provides a much-needed mechanism for reinforcing the learning process, bringing us back time and again to experience our feel-good moments until we've developed appropriately.

> *"Positive emotions have a clear psychology: they broaden people's mindsets; and that's beneficial, not in that particular moment, but in the longer term. If you've had more of those moments—those "broadened awareness" moments—you've accrued more resources that end up filling out your survival toolkit. It's an investment in the future. If we look only for the evolutionary advantage in the moment that you experience it, you won't see it. To be able to see the evolutionary advantage of positive emotions, you need to take that longer view– a developmental view."*

Positive emotions, it turns out, have short-term benefits too. In pioneering work with UC Berkeley psychologist Bob Levenson, Barbara identified the so-called "undoing effect", where positive emotions can be explicitly shown to sometimes counteract some harmful physiological changes that negative emotions have induced, acting *"as a sort of reset button to bring us back down to our baseline calm levels".*

But it is one thing to identify specific, beneficial, physiological mechanisms, or even finally develop a satisfactory evolutionary argument for something that we all know we have in the first place, it's quite another thing entirely to ponder what all of that might imply for our daily lives.

After all, if positive emotions are nature's way to help us learn important lessons for our long-term survival, it's hardly unreasonable to wonder if experiencing more of them, more regularly, will make us better equipped to cope with whatever challenges chance throws our way. Perhaps we can find a way to knowingly and actively enhance our own emotional development to our long- *and* short-term advantage? The answer, according to Barbara, turns out to be a resounding "yes".

> *"We have so much more capacity to regulate our emotions than we give ourselves credit for. We often think of emotions like the weather—they just happen. But, especially with positive emotions, we have a lot of choice about whether to let them emerge and bloom or just blow right past them because we're too busy doing something else. Positive emotions are particularly fragile. They are not as potent or powerful as negative emotions, and the initial seeds of them, in a way, are easy to overlook."*

That certainly sounds reasonable enough. But what, concretely, should be done? How do we let our positive emotions bloom?

> *"We had a few failed attempts at trying to create interventions that would raise people's positive emotions on a daily basis. It was humbling to realize that people's emotional personalities don't change very readily.*
>
> *"Then, serendipitously, I happened to be in a faculty seminar on integrative medicine and was introduced to some work on what's called 'Metta meditation', or 'loving-kindness meditation'. A huge light bulb went off for me: I could use this to test my theory!*

"That has been really fruitful for my research lab. We've found that people can, indeed, increase their positive emotions—not in a whopping way, but in a subtle upward shift in everyday mild positive emotions.

"What seems to be especially important are feelings of positive connection with other people. What we've discovered, even in interventions that don't rely on meditation—that just ask people to reflect on their moments of connection with others on a daily basis—is that this leads to upward shifts in positive emotions and associated changes in cardiovascular health."

Poets have known for millennia that connecting with others is good for one's heart. At long last, the scientists are now starting to appreciate it too.

The Conversation

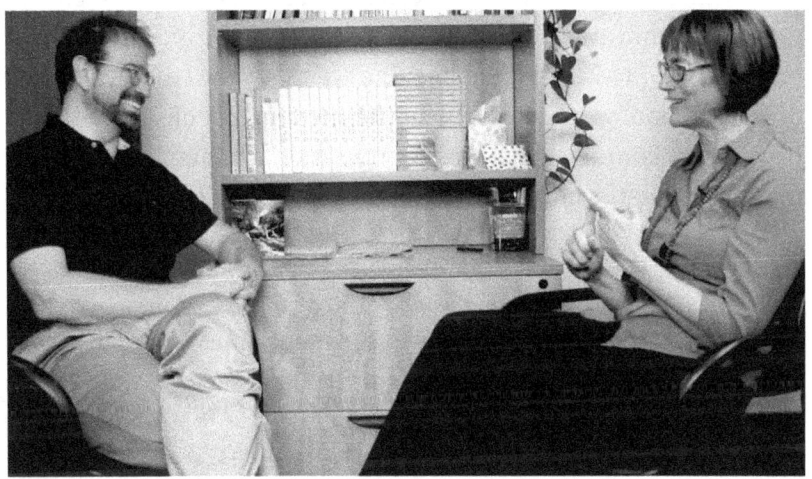

I. Psychological Beginnings
Towards social psychology

HB: How did your interest in psychology begin?

BF: My interest in psychology started in high school. Not exactly for the most highbrow reasons: my older sister was a psychology major and I wanted to be just like her. She was six years older and was doing graduate work in psychology at the time. I took a high school psychology course, which was pretty rare back then. I had a great teacher for that, which sparked my interest in the subject.

HB: What did this teacher do, exactly?

BF: Well, we did a lot of hands-on experimentation. We had our own Skinner box and trained our own rats. We conducted social-psychological experiments.

There were probably about 20 of us in the class—a very small class, with a great, hands-on instructor.

HB: So presumably you then went off to college with the goal in mind of studying psychology.

BF: Yes. But I had a good friend who was just a couple years ahead of me. He was a psychology major and it just wasn't for him. He told me, "*Do anything **but** be a psychology major.*" So I really tested myself and took chemistry, economics and many other courses. I did well in those classes but I was just so drawn to psychology.

HB: So you came back.

BF: Yes. I had tried other things, but I realized that psychology was really for me. At the end of that experience, there was no question that those were the ideas that I wanted to be thinking about by that point.

HB: And when you came back to psychology, did you have a particular orientation in mind? Were you thinking about abnormal psychology or social psychology? How did that develop?

BF: Well, I went to Carleton College, a small, liberal arts college in Northfield, Minnesota. There were about four faculty members in psychology; and all of social psychology, personality psychology, and clinical psychology was represented by one faculty member, Neil Lutsky. He was my mentor (we still stay connected).

Those were the courses I really liked, and I knew that I wanted to do something in social psychology. I wasn't so interested in the clinical side of clinical psychology. It's not that I don't care about people's suffering and outcomes, but I realized that I was just much more drawn intellectually to *How does this work?* rather than, *What can I do to make it better?*

My natural orientation is centred on mechanisms: how to unpack why humans are the way they are. I realized my questions were really basic science questions.

HB: Do you think that you would have had a similar career trajectory today, when there is so much more emphasis placed on cognitive science and neuroscience?

BF: That's a great question. I haven't really thought about that. I probably would have started off with much more of a biological focus, which I've developed over the years, maybe starting as a postdoc in psychophysiology. I feel like psychology, as a field, is integrating so rapidly with a more biological approach, and having that knowledge and awareness as a strength early on would be really helpful, whether it's neuroscience or immunology.

There are a lot of people who say, "*If I could start over, I would do neuroscience.*" I think the brain is fascinating, but I'm sometimes concerned that in all of our love of neuroscience, we're sometimes forgetting about the body. The body is very significant, and is obviously deeply related to the brain. Part of our wisdom is in the body. It's exciting for me to be able to be revealing some of that.

HB: Was that a view that you remember becoming aware of at a particular time? Was there some particular point in your academic career when you started thinking, *"Hey, this is all kind of together—the brain and the body influencing one another"*? Was there a particular "road to Damascus" moment for you about the link between the two?

BF: As a field, social psychology has gone through many different phases of self-concern about its overall relevance. Social psychologists naturally believe what they do is fascinating and interesting, but when I was in graduate school, there was a constant preoccupation with making it relevant, connecting more to health, illness and biology.

That's why I sought out the postdoc that I did, which allowed me to get training in psychophysiology to begin to make that clear bridge to health.

HB: So let's get back to your career—I had left you in Minnesota as an undergraduate a few moments ago. Before you did your postdoc, you presumably went to graduate school. How did that happen?

BF: I had a good opportunity as an undergraduate to do research with my mentor, Neil Lutsky. His area, at the time, was bridging between social psychology and personality psychology: how we perceive other people's character and personality traits.

I worked a lot on that; and at that time I thought that was what I wanted to do. I applied to schools where there were faculty members who did that kind of work, and ended up at Stanford.

In the end, my interests changed somewhat, but that's how I first decided that I wanted to be a social psychologist. At the time, I did have a glimmer of thinking *"Maybe I'll be an organizational psychologist"* (at the time it was called "industrial organizational psychology"), but after doing an independent study on that work, it seemed to me that that area of psychology was lagging behind social psychology—it was taking what was known in social psychology and applying it. So I thought to myself, *"I might as well get training in social psychology so I can be ahead of the curve."*

Questions for Discussion:

1. What are the strengths and weaknesses of taking a wide variety of courses outside of your core interests at the undergraduate level? Do you think that doing so should be common practice for most people?

2. How would you define "social psychology", exactly?

II. Emotions, Scientifically
From endings to moments of intensity

HB: When I was an undergraduate, there was this prevailing attitude that those who study psychology do so because they are consumed by their own personal problems that they're trying to solve—that was the stereotype, anyway.

BF: The "me search".

HB: Exactly. But what you're describing to me seems clearly motivated in a very different direction indeed: quite outward-looking and positive. You're not looking so much at the abnormal aspect of the human condition, but rather the human condition writ large. How common is that, do you think?

BF: My first love was with science: the idea that you can answer questions, working on the frontier of knowledge: *we don't know this so let's design a study to figure this out*. It's fascinating. It's one thing to be consuming the results of science, and a totally different game to be producing them. I just found that to be very intellectually gratifying.

My interest in emotions—which grew in graduate school and my postdoc—simply fits into this framework, although sometimes people assume there were special motivations.

People have asked me, "*You study positive emotions, positive psychology. Is this because you've had this extraordinarily happy childhood and everyone was bubbly and upbeat all the time?*"

And I say, "*Absolutely not*." I grew up in Minnesota, in a very stoic, Nordic household. There was no discussion of emotion and very little expression of emotions.

More generally, in psychology at the time, there was very little study of emotions either. It was just not a target of scholarly work in the 20th century until the late 1980s. It had been part of psychology at the initial 'get-go' a hundred years earlier with William James, but then Behaviourism shut the door on internal experiences as being a legitimate focus of study.

HB: It was considered just irrelevant?

BF: Yes: just lights on the machine—inconsequential. Then later, as the science of psychology was waking up to the idea that emotions can be studied, I came across it and thought, "*What is this emotions stuff?*"

It just wasn't part of the lexicon of our family conversations, for example, in the same way that my kids are exposed to them. I think our culture has changed so much in terms of our perception of a parent's job as "emotion-coaching" or "emotion-socialization". That wasn't even on the radar screen for my parents.

HB: Let's return to your graduate school days at Stanford for a moment. Tell me about your PhD thesis and then the postdoc you were talking about earlier.

BF: My PhD thesis was centred on an idea that came out of an undergraduate class I had, again, with Neil Lutsky. It was focused on "the psychology of endings", trying to understand what the endings of situations—the endings of relationships, the endings of life—have in common. I also worked with Laura Carstensen, who works in social gerontology. Central to her work is that late in life people start to prioritize emotions in their social interactions.

I was noticing that this happens at other endings too, like when people are graduating from college and are generally not interested in making new friends, preferring to spend time with someone they know well instead.

HB: They don't want to invest time in trying to establish a new relationship that they couldn't give sufficient time to.

BF: Exactly. That was my dissertation: *How any social ending creates the same kind of social behaviour that you see in late life.*

That debunked some early theories in social gerontology, which were centred on how older people are withdrawing from the social world "in preparation for death".

HB: I see. So this way you could point to previous precedents at other stages of life.

BF: That's right. Laura Carstensen's work had already challenged this view of "withdrawal", while my dissertation was an early piece of evidence to show that it's *endings* that do this—it's nothing about age, per se. It's just that endings tend to coincide with age.

That led to some work that I did with Danny Kahneman on what we call, "the peak-end" rule. When people think back on past emotional experience and sum it up, they refer to its peak emotional intensity and how it ended. Those two moments—those two snapshots—end up characterizing it, and they neglect the duration of the event, or some other aspects of it.

HB: And I can also imagine that, if they're over-emphasizing some particular aspects (like the peak or end), then they may also be misremembering other aspects.

BF: Yes, indeed; and we've done studies that show that. Even if something is objectively, say, more painful overall, if it has an improved ending, then you will probably be more likely to repeat it than something that was shorter and had a bad ending. People do make cognitive errors because they extract the peak and the end.

HB: Do they learn at all through this process? After having experienced, say, four different endings, by the fifth time, are you any better at decision-making, by some objective procedure?

BF: Great question. I don't know that. We didn't do the studies on whether people learn. We were just able to document that this is a reliable effect. And that's what got me interested in emotion: seeing these emotional hotspots, the ways our memory tracks emotion. That's what first got me interested in doing a postdoc in emotions.

HB: What surprised you during this early work on emotions?

BF: What surprised me, and what changed how we collect people's self-report of their emotional experiences to this day, is that people are generally not very good at remembering or integrating all their emotional experiences. So now we don't ask people, *"What's all the gratitude you felt today?"* Instead we ask them, *"How intense was the most intense moment of gratitude?"*

We try to get a representative snapshot of what people's emotions were like by just grabbing those peaks, because we know that those are more reliably recalled.

Questions for Discussion:

1. Can you give an example of how your behaviour towards others changed due to an anticipated "ending"?

2. Might growing up in a particularly "unemotional" environment also help pique someone's curiosity about the importance of emotional experiences?

III. Positive vs. Negative Emotions
Evolutionary conundrums

HB: Let's talk now about positive emotions. Perhaps an obvious way to set it up is to contrast them with negative emotions. We have some sense of where negative emotions come from, evolutionarily: you see a woolly mammoth coming towards you, you're fearful, and your body engages in some corresponding physiological response.

You may distrust people, you may get angry with people, and all of that has some associated physiological effect. It's not difficult to understand how these things are tied to our survival. But on the positive side, it's a lot harder to imagine how they might have actually come about.

BF: Exactly. That was the puzzle that drew me in. We had these templates for understanding the evolutionary value of emotions. As the science of emotions began to develop, there was kind of a "cookie cutter" template used for all emotions, which was: emotions promote specific action tendencies, which had helped our ancestors survive threats to life and limb.

And if you use that for understanding the evolutionary value of emotions, it's easy to just leave the positive emotions out. There were theories of emotion that were saying, "*This is how emotions evolved*", that didn't even *mention* positive emotions, which I find pretty amusing, given their obvious existence.

HB: And their obvious importance in most people's lives.

BF: Exactly.

What I did in my early work is to point out that we can't use the same theoretical framework to understand the value of positive emotions. In particular, the timescale is different. Whereas the adaptive value of a negative emotion is during the moment of threat—preparing you to do some action that is evolutionarily advantageous—

HB: —getting really worried because a woolly mammoth is around the corner, say—

BF: Exactly. But with positive emotions, there's no clear action tendency that's going to save your skin right at that moment, because, most often, there is no threat.

I argued that they have a clear psychology: they broaden people's mindsets. And that's beneficial, not in that particular moment, but in the longer term. If you've had more of those moments—those "broadened awareness" moments—you've accrued more resources that end up filling out your survival toolkit.

HB: It's an investment, then.

BF: That's right: it's an investment in the future. If we look only for the evolutionary advantage in the moment that you experience it, you won't see it. To be able to see the evolutionary advantage of positive emotions, you need to take that longer view—a developmental view.

HB: This reminds me of other sorts of behaviour that we do. Mothers spend an enormous amount of time with their newborns. This is a huge investment of time, energy, and resources. It certainly doesn't benefit the mother in the short term: it's a huge effort.

And this seems analogous to what you're talking about here, to the extent you don't see any immediate returns from it whatsoever. When it comes to caring for one's young, some say that we're "genetically disposed to doing so," but it seems to me that that's just begging the question.

BF: Yes, it's kind of circular.

HB: So it seems to me that this notion of an investment for positive emotions could be another example of a well-established phenomenon. Do these sorts of positive-emotion experiences exist in other species as well? Or is this somehow uniquely human?

BF: Certainly, other positive emotions can be seen in mammals at least, in terms of play. There is even some evidence that there are vocalizations in rats that seem to be like laughter. They happen with tickling, and when there is joviality. These are ultra-high frequency sounds, not audible to the human ear, but with the right recording devices we can detect them. There are entire research programs that try to assess this more concretely, determining if it's equivalent to an expression of positive emotion in animals.

There is certainly play that goes on in other mammals, too, that ends up looking like an investment in future behaviour. There are certain kinds of manoeuvres that juveniles of a certain squirrel species will do only in play—I think it's called "jinking"—where they catapult themselves on to a flexible branch and then go off into another direction. As adults they never do that unless it's a survival manoeuvre.

HB: So they're training themselves, prepping themselves for that eventuality.

BF: Exactly. It's something that's part of the play, and then becomes useful at a later point.

HB: This is what I was really going for, as I'm sure you understood. I'm looking for examples of this sort of theoretical framework that might apply to other cases, other situations. If the same sort of investment and broadening can apply, not only to humans but actually to some circumstances for other species, that strikes me as some additional evidence that you're on the right track.

BF: That's where I started with this theory. I was looking at some of the animal literature. Another way to incorporate evolutionary principles in the argument is to more generally appreciate how we might develop resources and skills to be better equipped to deal with adversity in the future. As humans, we've invented education for that, but positive emotions assure that you develop in that way just because it's rewarding.

Pleasant experiences themselves induce you to repeat that pleasant experience. It's like a sugar-coating that brings people back to the educational moment. You play because it's fun, and in playing you learn things. There are ways in which the hedonically positive aspect of positive emotions keeps bringing us back.

Now, it certainly gets humans into trouble as well through addiction to drugs, gambling and so forth. All of that is based on an exploitation of the positive-emotion system.

HB: Well, you're not responsible for that. You're responsible for giving me an evolutionary framework that makes sense. You can't stop people from going to Vegas all the time.

BF: Exactly. That's not my job.

Questions for Discussion:

1. What does Howard mean, exactly, when he says that the explanation of "being genetically disposed to doing something" seems to him to be "begging the question"?

2. If formal education is simply a collective form of "broaden and build", to what extent should it be explicitly design to provoke a positive emotional response in order to be successful?

IV. Positive Psychology Emerges
Examining human flourishing

HB: What was the response to all this when you were developing it? Was there an immediate *Yes, Barb is on the right track*, or *This is irrelevant; we've heard all this before* or something else entirely?

BF: There certainly wasn't the sentiment that *We've heard all this before*, because there was very little work done on positive emotions. I think it generated quite a lot of interest. One of my senior colleagues said, "*Gosh, I wish I'd have thought of that*", which I took as the greatest compliment. It captured a lot of interest in this new area called "positive psychology", which came along afterwards; and it helped make people realize that positive aspects are important.

HB: Is *positive psychology* necessarily linked to positive emotions, or is it in contradistinction to *abnormal psychology*? How is positive psychology actually defined?

BF: It's typically more in contrast to clinical psychology. The basic idea is that we've used the great scientific tools of our field to understand human misery. Let's now use those same tools to understand human flourishing, or functioning at a really high level. Positive emotions are one topic under the umbrella of this psychology.

The way I see it—I see everything through the lens of emotions now after all this time—is that positive emotions are the fuel, or the engine, that drives flourishing and well-being, by evolutionary design.

Early in my career, people were very excited by the theoretical ideas. I would publish things, and I'd hear responses like, *Hey, that's really cool—love that!* For the first, I'd say, 15 years or so, I just thought to myself, *Round of applause. It's doing great.*

As the field has grown and positive psychology grabs a lot more attention, people are becoming much more cautious and want to make sure everything that's said is right. Now I have my own merry band of detractors.

HB: That sounds like you're the victim of your own success to some extent, which is presumably a natural consequence of developing a key insight that gives rise to an entirely different way of looking at things. Once other people rush in, all sorts of subtleties will emerge, and people will start arguing over smaller and smaller details and definitions.

BF: Yes. It's just par for the course at this stage.

Questions for Discussion:

1. Do you think that properties like "human flourishing" or "well-being" will ever be rigorously defined objectively?

*2. To what extent does establishing disciplinary boundaries between areas such "positive psychology" and "clinical psychology" make sense? To what extent do those boundaries **not** make sense?*

V. Broaden and Build

A thesis emerges

HB: You speak of the "broaden-and-build" aspect of positive emotions, the notion that positive emotions are essential to our evolutionary growth in so far as they enable us to have a framework for doing all sorts of future activities that are fundamental to both our flourishing and our survival.

Without those, without the ability to socialize, without the ability to get along, we presumably wouldn't have developed language, society, and all these other things that are awfully good for us to have done. In short, we would just be running away from those woolly mammoths.

Is that a fair summary, you think?

BF: Yes. The whole purpose of the broaden-and-build theory is to explain the form and the function of positive emotions, their psychological shape and what value that had.

HB: So now there is also the question of comparing the value and extent of positive and negative emotions. Is there some meta-theory that says they should be in an ideal balance of some sort?

BF: One thing that we know clearly from a solid foundation of work is that there is a very strong negativity bias. Measure for measure, negative is stronger than positive in terms of the emotions.

In a way, the negative emotions scream out at us, while the positive emotions whisper. That makes really good sense from an evolutionary perspective in that if negative emotions are really about surviving the moment and positive emotions involve taking advantage of an opportunity so you might grow and become a better person in the future, negative emotions should trump positive emotions.

If we're here having this great conversation and that woolly mammoth comes through the window, we should stop.

So, in that sense, survival trumps investment in the future, which is the logic behind the negativity bias. In order to flourish, then, and really be at higher levels of mental well-being, a ratio of positive to negative emotions needs to be higher than 1:1, because at the level of 1:1, the negative emotions will just run roughshod over the positive ones.

There is research to suggest that the typical ratio across all people is 2:1. That is, people tend to have twice as many positive emotions as negative emotions. Our attention is always drawn to negative emotions, but in terms of day in and day out, people who are reasonably healthy typically have about twice as many positive emotions as negative ones. People who are clinically depressed, dealing with anxiety disorders, tend to be 1:1 or lower. This is just descriptive research.

What we found was that people who are flourishing, doing really well in life, tend to have ratios of 3:1, 4:1 or 5:1—appreciably above that 2:1 norm. That seems to be characteristic of people who are doing really well in life.

Questions for Discussion:

1. What does Barbara mean, exactly, when she says, "This is just descriptive research"? What do you think she is intrinsically contrasting it with?

2. Can "doing really well in life" be objectively assessed in a meaningful way?

VI. Emotional Measurement
Searching for objective criteria

HB: This leads directly to the question of how we might, on an individual basis, be able to improve that ratio. I'm going to defer that question for a moment, and will instead move towards a more detailed explanation of what we're actually measuring, scientifically.

I can imagine that a common type of response you might be receiving from those outside of your specific field might be something like, "*I can see that there is some broad-based way that you can justify, on an evolutionary basis, the fact that we have, and like to have, positive emotions. But what can we actually **do** with this? And how does all this tie in with physiological aspects that you were talking about earlier in terms of the integrated system of the entire body? Can we actually measure anything concretely?*"

BF: There are all kinds of ways to measure emotions. The key is to recognize that emotions are a complex system that is both mind and body at once. We can infer the presence of an emotion by triangulating on it from a number of perspectives. People's self-reports about what they are experiencing are a vital piece of that, but just one piece. We'll look at facial expressions. We'll look at observer reports. We'll measure physiological responses, in terms of cardiovascular change or changes in biochemistry.

When we're doing laboratory studies, there are typical ways that are used to reliably induce positive emotions in the laboratory. We tend to work with mild positive emotions, which I actually think is a strength of our approach. It's hard to bring the really extreme positive emotions like at the birth of a child or winning a lottery. You're not bringing those events into the laboratory.

HB: There'd be a lot of money in that if you could do it, though, I imagine.

BF: But you know what? The research shows that what matters about positive-emotion experience is the frequency, not the intensity. Intensity is great for highs every once in a while, but your day-in-day-out frequency of mild positive emotions is actually far more important than having a few really intense moments.

HB: When you say "important", what do you mean, exactly?

BF: Important in terms of well-being, flourishing, and maintaining mental health. We bring those mild positive emotions into the lab in very beguilingly simple ways: showing people short video clips of baby animals or beautiful nature scenes, or giving people an unexpected gift, like a small bag of candy. We don't let them eat it on the spot, so we know that any effect we might detect is not related to a sugar high. They take it away as an unexpected gift.

The unexpected gift, the video clip, sometimes writing about a positive memory: all those different techniques are used. Then we measure what happens to the scope of people's thinking right after that. There are some aspects of the "broaden-and-build" theory that you can test in a laboratory: *How does it change how the brain works in that moment? How does it change what happens in terms of physiology, in terms of undoing negative emotion or agitation?*

Other aspects of the theory you can't test in the laboratory, almost by definition, such as the "build" effect, this incremental effect.

HB: Right, because you don't have enough time to wait.

BF: Yes. So in that case, we repeatedly measure people's self-reports at day's end, over weeks and weeks.

HB: These are longitudinal studies, then?

BF: Yes. We have longitudinal studies where people get used to, every night, reporting what was the greatest amount of, say, 20 different emotions that they experienced—the greatest amount of anger, irritation, annoyance, gratitude, appreciation. They get used to reviewing their day in that way. We find that just simply doing that doesn't change people's emotions over time, but it's a good benchmark.

We're not asking people what some other researchers do, which is, *"Tell me about your emotions in general. Think back to the last month, what did you usually feel?"*

I don't think people can answer that question accurately: they just make things up. Or they make things up that are probably consistent with their views of their own personality.

In my experience, you get much more variability if you ask people questions closer to the size and shape of an emotion which is very short lived. We try to get them at the end of their day.

Other people use what's called "Ecological Momentary Assessment", where you regularly text people and ask, *"What are you feeling right now?"*

There are pros and cons to either approach. Each of them misses a lot of the emotional experience. I prefer the end of day reports because you can't realistically text people 100 times in one day—they would run from your studies screaming. You might ask them five times, and who knows whether or not those five moments are representative.

HB: How do you quantify emotions? You talk about a "stronger" emotion and a "milder" emotion. I can understand that intuitively. The birth of a child is obviously a very intense emotion compared to getting a bag of candy (unless it's really remarkable candy), but is there a way that you can quantify this more rigorously?

BF: It's not a perfect quantification, because each person's frame of reference is her own. Sometimes people will use a scale that's anchored with "the greatest amount in my entire life" versus "just a little bit" or "none".

We tend not to use "the greatest amount in my entire life" anymore because then people just avoid that completely and just work instead with the small part of a scale. We use a zero to four scale, from "none" to "a great deal" or "very intense" depending on whether we're trying to get frequency or intensity.

HB: I guess what I have in mind is a sort of futuristic polygraph test, where someone is able to say, "*I can see that you're very excited*" because they've hooked me up to some contraption and my pupils are dilated or whatever.

Is there a way, very crudely, that one can say, "*I can see this person's pulse is racing*" (or whatever)—there are some sort of objective physiological changes that enable me to quantify this as, say, a $7/10$ on the emotions scale?

BF: Well, there is a great wish for there to be some physiological measure that we could put on your brain, or measure on a polygraph that **is** the emotion. But there is no such thing. There isn't for negative emotions, there isn't for positive emotions.

We know now that this reductionist approach that just says, "*What your body is doing tells you what an emotion is doing*" is ill-fitting, because your body has many jobs. It's not just an emotion readout mood ring. It's digesting, helping you move from place to place, and so forth—all at the same time.

There is no biological measure that's going to be a one-to-one map with emotions. That is why people's self-reports are priceless: consciousness is a great integrator. Obviously, people have reasons that sometimes affect their ability, or their willingness, to report what they're feeling in a straightforward way.

HB: But if you have enough people and enough studies...

BF: Right. There is certainly noise in that measure, but it's one of the most effective measures, especially if you get it at a fine temporal resolution. There are ways to improve the measurement. It's certainly not perfect, but it allows science to progress.

How you know it's capturing something is that people's day-to-day emotion reports are accurately predicting theoretically hypothesized changes in cardiovascular function, or changes in gene expression in the immune system.

If it were all just people giving you the reports you want to hear, well, that wouldn't explain why their hearts are reacting in the way that they do.

HB: There is something objective going on, then, but it's certainly not a one-to-one map that you can easily single out.

BF: Yes, exactly.

Questions for Discussion:

1. What does Barbara mean, precisely, when she talks about distinguishing between frequency and intensity of emotional experiences?

2. Do you think that one day we will be able to construct a highly accurate "emotion polygraph test"? Why or why not?

VII. The Undoing Effect
A side benefit of positive emotions

HB: This brings me to "the undoing effect". My sense is that if I am under a lot of stress, or if I'm really angry, there is a corresponding deleterious effect on my body, at least if I am experiencing this sort of thing very often. That is, there are physical manifestations of my anger or stress that are not in my best interest.

My understanding is that you've done studies that have illustrated that there is a possibility of, to some extent, redressing or reversing at least some of this negative effect—undoing the harm done—by submitting oneself to increased amounts of positive emotions. Is that right?

BF: This was actually the first finding that I had on what positive emotions might be capable of doing that served as the kernel that then led to the development of the "broaden-and-build" theory. This came from an idea of one of my other former mentors, Bob Levenson, who is well known for his work on discovering what the bodily signatures of different emotions are.

In doing that early work, he had found that sadness seems to have one particular autonomic signature, fear another, and anger another. In that work it looks like positive emotions have none: they're not registering in peripheral physiology.

But, in an early chapter, he said, *"Maybe that's because we're looking in the wrong time and place. Maybe positive emotions don't look like they have a signature if we compare to a neutral baseline, but if we start out when people are feeling particularly anxious, then perhaps positive emotions—while not doing anything specific in the cardiovascular system, say—might be able to undo activation in that system. Perhaps positive emotions function as a sort of reset button to bring us back down to our baseline calm levels."*

We tested that in a number of different ways. And it looks to be the case that, if you are experiencing a negative emotion that is no longer useful—

HB: —the woolly mammoth has left the building, say.

BF: Exactly; then if you have the choice to continue to ruminate about that woolly mammoth, focus on something neutral or focus on something positive, the thing that is going to get you to reset the fastest is focusing on something positive. That is *the undoing effect* of positive emotions.

What I used to think, right when we first discovered that work, was that perhaps that was the function of positive emotions: to be these "undoers" of excessive negative emotions. When I tried to pull together a proper evolutionary argument on what positive emotions are good for, I came to the conclusion that this was a byproduct of this "broadening and building" effect more than the function itself.

Positive emotions are states that we experience in many different contexts, not just in the context of negativity, so we need to make sense of *all* the different ecological situations in which we experience them.

HB: I suppose that you can imagine that, from an evolutionary standpoint, such an explanation would only work if humans had this natural tendency to have a surfeit of negative emotions, so that it would be somehow vital for us to have this regularly cleansing effect that positive emotions could provide.

But, as I understand it, that's actually *not* the case. Most people aren't constantly thinking of woolly mammoths when woolly mammoths aren't actually there, which seems to suggest that in order to properly understand the evolutionary role of positive emotions we have to look somewhat deeper.

BF: Exactly.

Questions for Discussion:

1. Have you personally experienced instances of "the undoing effect" of positive emotions?

2. How are the concepts of "necessary" and "sufficient" involved in the logical structure of how Barbara determined that "the undoing effect" is a byproduct of the "broaden and build" aspect of positive emotions, rather than evidence of their primary evolutionary function?

VIII. Taking Charge

Cultivating positive emotional states

HB: I can imagine that somebody reading all this might say, *"That all sounds pretty good to me. Maybe I can help myself by focusing more on my positive emotions. Maybe I should meditate. Maybe I should try to have a different attitude as I go through life. Maybe that will have some significant physiological effect on me, for both my body and my brain."* Is that a reasonable response?

BF: Yes, definitely. We have so much more capacity to regulate our emotions than we give ourselves credit for. We often think of emotions like the weather—they just happen. But especially with positive emotions, we have a lot of choice about whether to let them emerge and bloom or just blow right past them because we're too busy doing something else. Positive emotions are particularly fragile. They are not as potent or powerful as negative emotions, and the initial seeds of them, in a way, are easy to overlook.

This is why mind training through meditation, we've learned in our studies, can actually be a really effective way to help people learn how to self-generate positive emotions and to recognize opportunities to do so.

I started studying meditation not to study meditation per se, but to test my theory. I really wanted to find out whether the "build" part of the "broaden-and-build" theory held water. And to do that, you have to essentially change people's emotional personality, change their daily diet of emotions by including more positive emotions.

We had a few failed attempts at trying to create interventions that would raise people's positive emotions on a daily basis. It was humbling to realize that people's emotional personalities don't change very readily.

Then, serendipitously, I happened to be in a faculty seminar on integrative medicine and was introduced to some work on what's called "Metta meditation", or "loving-kindness meditation". A huge light bulb went off for me: *I could use this to test my theory!*

I was emboldened by the fact that Richard Davidson and others had begun to do serious scientific work on "mindfulness meditation", and I thought I'd just swap in a different kind of meditation: one that has a specific aim, or intention, of cultivating warm and tender emotions.

That has been really fruitful for my research lab. We've found that people can, indeed, increase their positive emotions—not in a whopping way, but in a subtle upward shift in everyday mild positive emotions.

That is what people can create in their lives. And that subtle shift leads to changes in resilience, resourcefulness, cardiovascular health, immune health, and so forth. It doesn't have to be a huge change. People aren't suddenly changing from being incredibly dour to extremely happy-go-lucky: they're just becoming slightly more upbeat, uplifted, cheerful versions of themselves.

And what seems to be especially important are feelings of positive connection with other people. What we've discovered, even in interventions that don't rely on meditation, that just ask people to reflect on their moments of connection with others on a daily basis, is that this leads to upward shifts in positive emotions and associated changes in cardiovascular health.

HB: Tell me about the time involved for this process, because you mentioned earlier that this works on a different timescale—a longer timescale—that is associated with the whole idea of broadening. That makes me think that there must be some kind of threshold for effects to occur. Two minutes is clearly not enough, while two years is probably more than plenty. I'm guessing that you have some sense as to how long you have to be doing this until you start seeing concrete effects.

BF: We've always done these tests with a certain "dosage" of meditation. We haven't done titration studies to determine what the minimum amount might be.

Our studies involve people in a six-week workshop on meditation where they attend a group class for one hour per week, and then we ask them to do home practice three to five times a week. They end up investing between 60 and 90 minutes in this practice over the course of a week, which is considerably less than what a lot of other meditation interventions ask for (often an hour per day).

The guided meditations that we've used are really short—15 to 20 minutes—and we typically find that we see these changes over a season: two and a half to three months from our first to second testing.

HB: OK, so now I'll ask you to speculate: do you have a sense as to what a minimal duration might be?

BF: When it comes to these micro-interventions I mentioned earlier—just reflecting on connection—we see that they're not as powerful as learning a meditation practice. But the effects are still observable.

Those people are investing less than a minute per day reflecting upon, *What were your three longest social interactions of today? How close did you feel? How attuned did you feel?*

We find that asking yourself those questions about connection leads to emotional changes and cardiovascular changes. One of my graduate students right now is doing work to figure out what these questions are actually doing. Are they changing the way people value their experience? Or are they nudging their behaviour in a different way? Maybe if I know that I'm going to have to answer that question every day, I'll be more predisposed to finding some connection.

We're going to see if it's more of a behavioural shift or a cognitive shift. That is where the state of the science is right now. Not everybody is into meditation, it's not going to be something that everyone is interested in investing time in.

But just reflecting on connection is something that we often don't do. We might do it on Thanksgiving or some other key moments of the year, but it has a real, positive effect if you take it up as a daily ritual.

HB: That makes me think of something you said before: that perhaps there is some sort of a hierarchy of positive emotions, and that this notion of connection might be at the very top of the hierarchy.

BF: Yes, that's what motivated me to write my second book, *Love 2:0*. I wanted to explore the idea that perhaps our experiences of shared positivity are more influential to our health than our solo experiences of positivity.

Not that those solo experiences aren't important as well, and can also lead to important developmental changes—they can—but it might be the case that there could be some real hierarchy, with shared positivity being like "super nutrients". If all positive emotions are nutrients, these are the broccoli, in a sense.

HB: From a 'person on the street', common sense, viewpoint, this is not so surprising, because love is something, broadly defined, that we find everywhere. It certainly is something that drives human societies. Everyone wants to talk to you about his or her personal experiences. The fact that this is so incredibly prevalent in our society—and, more broadly, in our species—might well be linked to the fact that it has such a significant effect on us.

BF: One of the things that I think is important to recognize is that in our culture we tend to think of love as finding that soul mate, that one relationship.

What's kind of sad about that is that for most adults—at least in the US—they've either never found that one person or have since lost that one person. Does that mean that there is no love in their lives and no connection?

I'm trying to lower the bar on what love is by describing it as these micro-moments of positive connection that we can have with people we know well, or even those we've never met before.

The value of the small positive connections we make in our community may contribute to a sense of feeling safe, feeling at home. Having lots of these micro-moment positive connections with people you don't even know may actually be just as powerful as the ones that strengthen your most important bond relationships.

HB: Again, it's a question about frequency trumping intensity: integrating the cumulative effects over a longer period of time.

BF: Exactly.

Questions for Discussion:

1. Do you meditate? Has this chapter influenced your beliefs regarding the possible physiological effects of meditation?

2. Do you think that just knowing that you will regularly be required to reflect on your connection with others is just as, if not even more impactful on our emotional states, than the very act of reflection itself?

3. Is our contemporary definition of "love" too narrow, on the whole?

IX. Responses

The perks and perils of relevance

HB: What has the response been to *Love 2.0* and this idea of these connections being supremely important to us?

BF: I think the reception has been good. I've got a number of colleagues who have been interested in sharing data that might be used to test things further. It's led to some neat projects.

It's inspired by my work with this meditation practice, "loving-kindness meditation". I think there is no accident that working on that led me to rethink my ideas about how love is working. What is it? How is it affecting the body and health?

That book was written to frame the kind of work I'd like to do in the next 20 years, whereas my first book, *Positivity*, was describing what I'd done during my first 20 years. I was hoping that it would be a more generative framework, and we're beginning to see the initial evidence of that.

HB: Clearly, scientifically, you're looking at how your colleagues respond, with an eye to how best to further develop your research agenda.

But one of the interesting aspects of your work, unlike, say, a cosmologist or a fish biologist, is that it resonates with a lot of people who are not necessarily scientists themselves.

Since you're talking about something so common to humanity and the human condition, there's a natural link there. I can imagine that would be very stimulating for you, being occupied with something that is so obviously relevant to so many people.

On the other hand, I can also imagine that it might sometimes be somewhat frustrating as well, finding yourself in the "self-help" section, with many assuming that you are simply going to tell them how to lead a fulfilled life by some straightforward 10 point plan. Is that a common experience for you?

BF: It is; and yet what a great opportunity to be doing science in an area that people care about. It's a wonderful opportunity, but it does create some funny tensions in places.

On the whole, though, it feels enormously gratifying to see people express interest in these topics. There was a time when "self-help" books were written by anybody but scientists. In the last ten years or so, psychologists have realized, *Wait a minute,* **we** *have something to say about this. Maybe we should have some offerings on that shelf too.*

So I'm not at all embarrassed to be in the "self-help" aisle. I actually think it's important that there be some evidence-based work there. Both of my books are written with a Part 1 and a Part 2.

Part 1 describes the science, Part 2 is the, *OK, if that's true, what do I do?* aspect of things. People can read them for what matters to them. I hope I can get people to be interested in the really cool stuff in the front part of the book that's about the science, but some people are more interested in going straight to the second part, saying to themselves, *OK, I buy all that, now what do I do?*

HB: It's a happy combination, because as a scientist it could have been the case, logically, that positive emotions could have been somehow disadvantageous. One could imagine, at least logically, that the sorts of things that people might like to hear are not actually what's going on, scientifically.

In other words, you began your scientific studies with an open mind, and it just so happens that we've come to the conclusion where we have this happy overlap that what makes us feel good is actually advantageous and we should be doing more of it (in moderation, in the right way, and so forth). And if that's the case, then there's even an argument that you might have a moral obligation to tell people about it.

BF: Yes. And that's part of what motivated my first book, *Positivity*. I felt like, *This is not just science anymore*. This is a little bit about life and how to live it; and people should know.

It did feel like a calling. I never would have imagined that I would write for a general audience when I envisioned my career early on. It wasn't on the list of things I thought I would do, but eventually I came to feel, *I find this is incredibly useful and important to know this; other people might too.*

It is also a very different kind of writing than writing research articles, and I found that enjoyable too. I see it as an extension of my teaching mission. I'm not just teaching students in my own university, I'm also teaching anybody who is interested.

There is one caution to what you are saying, though: just because positive emotions have these benefits for us in terms of building our resources and helping us become better versions of ourselves, that doesn't mean that our attempts to self-generate them aren't sometimes going to backfire.

I describe this in *Love 2.0* as contrasting "authentic" or "genuine" positive emotions with the "wishful thinking" positive emotions that people sometimes exhibit—"*No, I'm feeling fine, I'm great*"— words you say to other people or yourself that can sometimes be pretty locked in as self-deception.

The key to seeing the difference between these "forced smile" versions of positivity and the genuine article is seeing how much they are filtering down into the body, into the ways you carry yourself, into your emotional calmness, into your ready social connection.

HB: Can non-specialists see the difference? Can a woman on the street be able to self-diagnose herself and say, "*Gosh, I thought I was self-generating these things properly, but in fact I wasn't*"?

BF: I think you can, to some degree, if you're willing to look in the right places. Does the day feel easier? Do I feel more capable? Do I feel like I'm growing in resilience? Maybe the answer is, *No, not really: I'm feeling really brittle*. Well, that's a sign right there.

In terms of registering the sincerity of other people's expressions of positivity, we're really good at that if we make eye contact. If we don't make eye contact with other people, research shows we're actually pretty cut off from that gut wisdom that tells us whether somebody is just telling a story.

HB: Why is that? What is it about eye contact?

BF: There is this great work by social psychologist Paula Niedenthal on what she calls the "Simulation of Smiles Model". When we make eye contact we immediately and automatically begin to mimic that facial expression. As we mimic that facial expression, we have a neural mimicry going on as well, which helps inform us as to what that smile might mean.

There is not just one kind of smile. There is the *I'm enjoying my chocolate totally oblivious to you* smile. There is the *we're sharing an experience* smile. There is the *I'm better than you* gloating smile.

Disambiguating all those different kinds of smiles is very difficult without making eye contact, while if you *do* make eye contact, you're much better at seeing and interpreting those subtle differences.

Other people are actually really good "mirrors" for us. If you think you're being positive, but you're not drawing other people in and seeing positivity on their faces, then it's probably not real.

It's subtle, because our culture—especially American culture—is very much focused on conveying messages like *Be happy! Don't cause problems! It's all good!*

But positive emotions are not meant to be a permanent veneer. All emotions are adapted to the extent that they fit the situation, and when they don't fit the situation—when a positive emotion, or a smile, is put on like a mask—it's not going to be effective.

Questions for Discussion:

1. What percentage of your outwardly expressed positive emotions would you say are true indicators of the way you are feeling?

2. Are there justified concerns for scientists writing self-help books, or is the bias against doing so merely an expression of academic snobbishness?

X. Personal Flourishing
Bringing it home

HB: I haven't known you any longer than an hour or so, but you seem to be somebody who's completely comfortable in her own skin with a reasonable good handle on her emotions. I'm wondering if all this emotions research has changed you personally.

BF: Definitely. As I was mentioning earlier, I didn't have much of an "emotional education" in my youth. I think there was a stretch where I was completely fascinated by the science, drawn into it, and at the same time, because of my love of science, I was well over the edge in becoming a workaholic.

By my late thirties, in the midst of seeking tenure and those sorts of things in academia that lead one to overdo it, the irony of it sunk in. Here I was studying flourishing mental health, and I wasn't sure I was flourishing myself: I wasn't sure my marriage was going to last if I kept on that path. I realized that I could really take lessons from my own work.

I thought to myself, *"If that's true, if flourishing people have this higher ratio of positive-to-negative emotions, then working 14-hour days in isolation is not going to lead to good places."*

I was really lucky that what pulled me back from the edge was the very work that was piling up on my desk. So I feel like I'm the first student of this work in terms of it making a difference in my life; and I'm really lucky in that way.

HB: And has your work, or your awareness of your work, also influenced the way you interact with your own children?

BF: Yes, I think it's made me a better parent too, especially when your kids are really young, and you find yourself saying, *"No, no, no, don't do that"* all the time.

Just having the awareness to say to myself, *You know what? I should say "yes" sometimes* is helpful, instead of always just being the "no" person. That's helped me to try to keep the right balance, to try to create the family rituals that keep fun stuff as part of our daily and seasonal routines.

I think about that a lot. My oldest is now in high school, and he's very much like me in terms of just being, as I was at that time, very scholarly focused. He's taking all these honours classes and then comes home and he does five hours of homework each night. I sit down with him and say, *"That's all great! I'm glad you're a great scholar, but what are you doing for fun?"*

HB: Does he listen to you?

BF: Not enough. I have to work on that in terms of getting him to take it seriously. I've talked to them so much about "upward spirals of growth", and he says, *"Yeah, yeah, upward spirals, Mom. I get it..."*

HB: *"Now let me get back to my work."*

BF: Exactly. I think he takes it to heart a little bit, but he's got to find his own areas of passion. I'm just trying to support that.

Questions for Discussion

1. Might some people regard engaging in scholarly activity as actually "having fun"? To what extent does this passage about Barbara's son reveal our sociological biases towards "educational activities" and the function of education in contemporary society?

2. To what extent does the natural "human element" of psychological research complicate that very research effort?

XI. Leveraging Positivity
Generating upward spirals

HB: Anything I missed? Anything you want to talk about that we haven't gotten to?

BF: I think we've discussed a lot of different areas. We covered how positive emotions make people more resilient, change the way the brain works, and help us grow and change.

The work that I'm doing right now in my research lab is centred on how to use what we know about positive emotions to support healthy lifestyle changes. One of the things that we're testing is an offshoot of the "broaden-and-build" theory, which is what I'm calling this "upward spiral" theory of lifestyle change.

Our positive emotions change us biologically in ways that turn up the volume on the positive-emotion system so that healthy behaviours become even more rewarding, which naturally knits us into a healthier lifestyle. The typical way that people try to make a change in their life in terms of health is using top-down willpower, saying, "*I **should** do this*". I'm trying to use what we know about the emotion system to create this non-conscious pull towards healthy behaviours.

That's what all of our current work is on: testing this "upward spiral" theory and seeing if you increase your positive emotions through one means—say, through learning how to meditate. Does that actually make other health behaviours, like being physically active or eating fruits and vegetables, more affectively rewarding? Do you get drawn and pulled in to taking care of the body in other ways?

HB: You mentioned this "loving kindness" meditation earlier. What is that, exactly, and how does it differ from other forms of meditation?

BF: It's an ancient Buddhist practice that can be done in a completely secular way. It hinges on this drumbeat of these phrases that you repeat to yourself. Some forms of meditation, like mindfulness meditation, have you keep your attention focused on the breath, and keep returning to the breath.

In this practice, you keep returning to these phrases, which are essentially wishes for another person's well-being or your own. The classic phrases go something like, *"May you feel safe"*, *"May you feel happy"*, *"May you feel healthy"*, *"May you live with ease"*.

It's not like there's any magic in those words, but a repetition of those phrases with the intention of creating that warm, tender, compassionate feeling towards the self and others, is what seems to drive it.

If people are interested in that, the website that goes along with *Love 2.0* is www.positivityresonance.com, which includes some short, guided meditations that people can sample and use as a base for learning more.

HB: How long do you do it for?

BF: The guided meditations that we use in our research that are on that website are about 15, maybe 20, minutes. We found that if people practice that three to four times a week, that seems to be all that you need to do to have your heart rhythms take note, have your immune system take note. It's not a huge investment, and it keeps me continuing to come back to the practice myself.

I've tried to do everything that I ask our research participants to do. I've learned meditation alongside our first research participants because I thought, *"Well, I can't be studying this if I don't know what it is."* That's how I started getting interested in meditation: through the science.

HB: Science can save your life.

BF: Yes, exactly. It saved mine.

HB: Well, Barbara, thank you very much for taking the time to talk with me and discuss your work. It's been a pleasure.

BF: Thanks. It's been fun.

Questions for Discussion:

1. *How do you think that "willpower" is related to positive emotions? Might our classic views of "willpower" need to be revised in light of the work of Barbara and other social psychologists?*

2. *Has this conversation increased your interest in harnessing the development of your own positive emotions?*

Continuing the Conversation

Readers interested in getting a deeper perspective on Barbara's views are encouraged to read her books: *Love 2.0: Finding Happiness and Health in Moments of Connection* and *Positivity: Top-Notch Research Reveals the 3-to-1 Ratio That Will Change Your Life.*

Critical Situations

A conversation with Philip Zimbardo

Introduction

Should Have Knowns

When you first start delving into Philip Zimbardo's infamous 1971 Stanford Prison Experiment, two words immediately pop to the surface.

The first is "classic". Nearly half a century after those six intense days in August when 24 summer students had rapidly metamorphosed into sadistic guards and riotous prisoners, the study has long established itself as one of the most famous experiments in the history of social psychology, standing firmly alongside Stanley Milgram's work a decade earlier as a formidable demonstration of the powerful effects of situational forces on human behaviour.

The second word, though, is "controversial". Ever since the results of the study were announced, there were strong voices raised against it on ethical, statistical and procedural grounds. Some said that the numbers involved were too small to prove anything, while others maintained that circumstances were so artificial as to naturally encourage the study's participants to role-play in the way they thought was expected by them. Meanwhile, several levelled serious criticism at Zimbardo's own role in the study, accusing him of sinking to an almost similarly depraved state as the "guards" by allowing such emotionally-damaging experiences to continue in the name of a scientific study.

What many might not appreciate, however, is that few can be harder on the renowned Stanford University social psychologist than he is himself, consistently recognizing his own profoundly unethical behaviour, together with the vital role his then-girlfriend, Christina

Maslach, played in convincing him to shut the study down 8 days earlier than planned.

> "She began to tear up. I asked her what the matter was and she got really upset. She said, *'I can't look at that!'* I started telling her about the dynamics of human nature and all that, and she just ran out.
>
> "At that point, I was stressed to my limit. I was not sleeping regularly. We ran out in front of Jordan Hall—it's now 10:30 at night—and I was yelling at her, saying, **'Don't you understand that there are dynamics here that have never been seen or studied before? Most experiments only last one hour, but these people are living and becoming prisoners and guards!'**
>
> "She just said, **'It's terrible what you're doing to these boys. They're not prisoners or guards. They're boys in your experiment. They are being mistreated. It's terrible what's happening'**.
>
> "I kept trying to re-frame it in terms of the dynamics of the situation, but she just said, **'I don't understand how you could see what I just saw and not react the way that I am reacting. I know you'**—she had been a TA of mine—**'You love students. You're a loving teacher. But this situation has changed you. You're not the person that I thought you were.'**
>
> "And then she told me, **'If this is the real you, I don't want to have a relationship with you'**. That was the clincher. That was like a slap in the face.
>
> "It was now eleven o'clock at night. I said, **'You're right. I will end this study tomorrow. Let's go to dinner and think about how I'm going to shut this down.'**

There's no point, then, in trying to convince Phil Zimbardo that he was involved in an unethical study, or that he became far too personally involved and lost his scientific objectivity. He knows that better than anyone.

> "I still feel guilty about it. I allowed evil to exist. In the breakdown of every one of those kids, I am as responsible as any of the guards, because I saw what was happening and didn't stop it."

But beyond the guilt and finger-pointing lie some terrifying yet crucial lessons. *What*, exactly, was going on? How could a group of largely pacifistic students quickly slip into the role of barbarous guards, mercilessly forcing their fellow students to perform shockingly degrading acts for their amusement? None of that seems possible to be waved away by appealing to simple notions of role-playing or a lack of scientific objectivity. These were real people who rapidly began wantonly degrading and humiliating their peers just for the hell of it. And the more they did it, the more entrenched they became in their role.

What is happening, it seems, is that people's behaviour is being strongly influenced by "situational effects". We're still ultimately responsible for our own actions, of course, but it's essential to recognize the enormously influential role played by the situational power structure around us and the systems that produces it.

So goes Phil's formal, academic, view of the underlying forces of social psychology. But suddenly, well over 30 years after the Stanford Prison Experiment, the textbooks came alive with a vengeance as the world is forced to grapple with horrific images of American servicemen and women abusing and humiliating Iraqi prisoners at Abu Ghraib.

> "Abu Ghraib was a replay of the Stanford prison study on steroids— exponentially worse. Things went on 12 hours every night for three months, and the few pictures that were shown publicly—a dozen pictures or so—were nowhere near the worst. I actually have access to a thousand of these images, which are truly horrendous: every different kind of degradation you can imagine, performed by American men and women, military police soldiers, on Iraqi prisoners in their charge, night after night for three months.
>
> "How could that happen for three months? When you see the pictures, you assume it must have taken place on just one night. So right away,

> *that means that somebody was not minding the store, that there was a systemic flaw.*
>
> *"The abuses only took place during the night shift. Not one abuse occurred during the day shift. That's a situational variable.*
>
> *"One of the motivations for evil is boredom. The worst abuses in the Stanford prison study were at night. The guards would come in, and they had eight hours to kill. The prisoners were sleeping, they had nothing to do, so they would wake them up and play with them.*
>
> *"At Abu Ghraib, Chip Fredrick and the other guards worked 12-hour shifts, from 4 pm to 4 am. Then, at 4 am at the end of the shift, he went to sleep in a prison cell in a different part of the prison, because the prison was always under bombardment. He never left the prison, so he was situationally-bound."*

You might think that, given the stakes involved and the likelihood of such horrific circumstances repeating themselves in the ongoing "war on terror" with an unequivocally catastrophic effect on everything from international opinion to troop morale, American authorities would pay more attention to the role of powerful situational forces.

But sadly, you'd be wrong.

> *"General Myers actually said, '****There is no evidence that it's anything but those individuals. Our army, our training is above that. There is no other evidence of such a thing happening anywhere else.****'*
>
> *"It turns out that was a lie. At the same time Abu Ghraib was happening, the same sorts of things were happening at a number of other prisons."*

Lying about the existence of a deeply troubling systemic malady is bad enough. But denying its existence while strongly helping it to come into being is quite another. Because it turns out that the authorities in question not only knowingly turned a blind eye to the illegal and profoundly immoral treatment of prisoners, they actually clearly encouraged it.

*"The pressure was coming down from Bush and all the military leaders at the top. Suddenly, military intelligence goes to the military police heads and says, '**Your guys have to take the gloves off. We need actionable intelligence. We need your guards to prepare the prisoners so that when we interview them, they will spill the beans.**' Essentially they were saying, 'Do whatever you have to do.'*

*"They're creating a new situation by saying, '**Do whatever you have to do. We don't care.**' In fact, not only, '**We don't care,**' but, '**We're never going to notice.**' Had the guards not taken the pictures, they could have done worse things. Nobody would have noticed. Nobody would have cared."*

During the mounting propaganda effort behind the American invasion of Iraq, then Secretary of Defense Donald Rumsfeld famously spoke of "known knowns, known unknowns, and unknown unknowns", owlishly attempting to differentiate between threats we are aware of, threats we can't predict and threats we can't even presently envision.

It goes without saying that he didn't mention the dangers posed by wantonly ignoring basic aspects of social psychology that we had discovered long ago.

But it turns out that those well might have been the greatest threats of all to American values.

The Conversation

I. Origins
Humble beginnings

PZ: My life began in the South Bronx, New York City, in 1933, during the Great Depression. I was born to George and Margaret Zimbardo, who were lovely parents. They were uneducated—neither of them even went to high school, let alone graduated from it. They were both of Sicilian background; their parents had immigrated to the United States from small towns in Sicily.

Both came from big families—my mother's family had 11 children, my father's family had 10 children. As in many Italian and Sicilian families, family was the core. There were four children in my family. I was the oldest, and I had two brothers and a sister.

But we were very poor. My mother's father was a shoemaker who had a shop in the Northern Bronx that I visited on occasion. In my father's family they were all barbers—my grandfather, uncles, and cousins. That was my father's trade too, but he hated it.

He should have been a prince. He was very handsome and very elegant. He was the first son after seven sisters, which meant that he was spoiled rotten. Even when he was an adult, his sisters would call him Giglio, which roughly translates to "little George".

Although he was totally uneducated academically, he was a genius in many ways. He was very musically gifted. He could play many instruments by ear—piano, violin, guitar, mandolin, especially. He could listen to a song—the theme from *The Godfather*, say—and, in 30 minutes he would be playing it.

HB: He probably never had any formal musical training either.

PZ: None whatsoever, as far as I know. He almost had perfect pitch.

In addition to that, he also had incredible mechanical abilities. He could make almost anything and would repair cars or broken radios. In fact, the only time he ever made money was during the Second World War when he opened a radio shop. You couldn't buy new radios at that time, so the only thing people could do was fix their old tube ones. He opened a radio store in the Bronx and we started to become better off.

He didn't want to be a barber, because he thought barbers were like servants because they wait on people. He thought people should be waiting on him, as his sisters had done. One day, he just quit and said, "*I'm not going to be a barber any more.*" Then, for a long period of time he did nothing, until he opened the radio store several years later.

We had a family of four and we were on what was called "Home Relief." But he didn't care. My father's main personality trait is what I would call complacence. He was happy with his life, whereas my mother would be crazy because we had no money. I don't know what you got from Home Relief, maybe $60 a week for four kids. Money was always a big issue. We never had enough.

I had an uncle, George—my mother's older brother—who was a bachelor and lived nearby. We were like his substitute family. He would come several times a week and bring us doughnuts, pastries, newspapers and so forth. He even set up a credit account at Charlie's Candy Store where we could each spend five cents a week, or something like that. So we always felt privileged because someone was looking after us, even though we were essentially poor.

We lived within our means—which meant, for example, you had pasta three times a week—big pasta with meatballs on Sunday, pasta with fish or just oil on Friday, and some other pasta on Wednesday. It was all good and fresh. None of us were ever fat. We were never over-nourished.

One thing my father did which was truly extraordinary was build a television set. The first television set was invented in 1946; and in 1947 he built his own TV from a wiring diagram, from scratch, entirely on his own. In 1947, we saw the World Series on an 8-inch screen and actually charged 25 cents to let people watch it with cookies and lemonade.

Another brilliant thing he did was to get a parabolic magnifying glass and put it right in front of the television, so you could see the picture—albeit slightly distorted—from all angles. Of course everybody said, *"George, I want one. Can you make me one?"* And he said, *"No, the challenge was to make one."* I pleaded with him, *"Dad, we could help here. Everybody wants one and we could really use the money."* But, he just said, *"The challenge was to make one, and that's it."*

HB: It was just for himself.

PZ: Yes, it was just a challenge for himself.

Another thing he used to do was buy old pianos and totally remodel them—refinish them, put French legs on them, put mirrors in front, sometimes emboss them with *"George Zimbardo & Sons"* in gold. Again, of course, people would ask, *"George, could you do that for me?"* And he would say, *"No, no. I did one. That's enough."* That made me crazy.

That's partly how I became interested, later in life, in the psychology of time perspective. My father lived in what I would call "the expanded present." He lived for the moment. He never thought about the future. He was content. He was satisfied with what he had.

HB: He probably didn't think about the past very much either.

PZ: Not at all. The past didn't exist to him. He never talked about the old ways; it was always a question of how to enjoy the present. He was obviously desirable at parties—he could sing, apparently he was a great dancer, he could tell stories, he could tell jokes, and he was charming. But he didn't fit as the father of a family of four.

My parents made a mistake—obviously, they got married too soon. My mother was very attractive—which, again, was probably part of his present-oriented perspective. They made love, had a baby, and all of a sudden he had to play the father role.

HB: I'm guessing that your mother didn't live in the expanded present. Presumably she couldn't afford to.

PZ: She never did. Her thing was, "*Life goes on.*" For her, life was about suffering until someday it'll get better. That was sad for me. As the oldest child, I was often the husband surrogate. If my father didn't come home until late, I would stay up with my mother listening to radio programs. We'd listen to Bob Hope and she'd tell me what the *double entendres* meant, these semi-sexual jokes, and that sort of thing. As a result, I essentially grew up faster than my age; and very often I would be instructed to take care of my younger brothers.

HB: So you were also a father surrogate, to some extent.

PZ: I was a father surrogate to my brothers, yes. We were all only roughly two years apart. I was a husband surrogate to my mother, and a father surrogate to the other kids. I would be the one to tell them to believe in Santa Claus or the Easter Bunny. At four or five, my parents told me they didn't exist and that I was going to find out sooner or later so it may as well be now, but together we were going to deceive the younger kids.

Those were formative experiences. As I said, a consequence of that for me was that I became excessively future-oriented. I could appreciate the fact that my father loved the present. A pasta dinner was not just eating pasta. He would take fifteen minutes to break up basil leaves, mix three different kinds of cheeses, cut up pieces of meatballs, and arrange it all in a certain way. We'd be dying because we couldn't start eating before he did. But at the same time, I could step back and appreciate his enjoyment of the present.

HB: You could? That seems quite remarkable to me under the circumstances.

PZ: I could appreciate it for him. I would think to myself, *If we had money, I could do that too. But we don't, and he doesn't care; and it's clear that we're never going to be successful with that mentality.*

It became obvious to me that school was the only way to get out of poverty—that is, being in school, doing well in school, was the way out. And school was clean and organized. There wasn't the chaos of living in a ghetto neighbourhood. There were simple rules: you did this and you got an A and you were the teacher's pet; you did that and on Friday you would get a special gift, like a pen, or a pencil, or something.

HB: Did you have a sense of what the best course of study was to move forwards?

PZ: No, it was just, *"Do well in school, get the best grades, and then move to the next level."*

At some point, after my father worked in the radio shop, he got into electronics. He realized that was a real career, and that he was good at it. He worked for some big companies as a wiring technician and then he became a foreman because, as I mentioned, he was charming and he knew how to work with people.

HB: On top of that, presumably he was also good at what he was doing.

PZ: Oh, yes. Whatever he was doing, he did really well. He was a craftsman, a Renaissance man. He took pride in the product.

It was then that we started to become moderately well off because he was working regularly, and my brother George was working with him.

When I graduated high school, he said to me, *"OK, now it's time to go to work."* I said, *"No, I have to go to college."* He told me that we couldn't afford it, and I literally had to get my high school teacher to come to dinner and advocate for me, saying, *"If he goes to college, he'll make more money."*

That worked, in part, but we still couldn't afford for me to go to college. So I went to Brooklyn College, which in those days was free. But then my father told me, *"If you're not bringing any money in, you can't take any money out. You have to get a job."*

So I became a concession boy in the St. James Theater on 44th St, on Broadway. I checked the hats and coats of the people coming in: we sold programs to the show, candy, and orangeade. I did that Monday through Thursday and two performances on Saturday, from the summer of my senior year in high school until my senior year in college.

When I went to Brooklyn College I was still living in the Bronx. I had to spend an hour and a half on the train to school, then on to Broadway, where I worked until 11pm, and I'd get home around midnight. I was working intensely, but I loved it. I loved show business, and I loved going to school.

Questions for Discussion:

1. To what extent were you able to simultaneously recognize and appreciate the weaknesses of your parents when you were a child? How unique do you think Phil's behaviour was at this time? How might his thoughts at the time have been influenced by his familial role as both "husband surrogate" and "father surrogate"?

2. How do you think that Phil's career would have evolved had Brooklyn College not been free at the time? Additional examples of how affordable post-secondary education strongly influenced the development of renowned academics can be found in **Democratic Lessons: What the Greeks Can Teach Us** *with Stanford University classicist and political scientist Josiah Ober and* **The Consolations of History** *with UCLA medieval historian Teo Ruiz.*

II. A Formative Quarantine
Developing social survival skills

PZ: I learned how to be a leader early on. And in any situation I was in—with one interesting exception, the year we moved to North Hollywood, California—I was always "the captain," "the president," "the vice-president,"—of my fraternity, of the track team, class elections, whatever it was.

And the reason was that, when I was five, I developed double pneumonia and whooping cough. Whooping cough is a very contagious disease, and I developed it at the same time as the pneumonia. I was a little, skinny kid, and the combination of those two things meant I could hardly breathe. I had to struggle for every breath.

Many poor children had lots of contagious diseases in those days because we all lived in close quarters and tenements, and if you did come down with one you had to go to a hospital on the East River in Manhattan called *Willard Parker Hospital for Children with Contagious Diseases*.

It was basically a huge quarantine base for tuberculosis, scarlet fever, whooping cough, and polio—there was a polio epidemic around that time as well. There were hundreds of kids and hundreds of beds.

This was 1938. There was no penicillin, no sulfa drugs, no treatment for any contagious disease—which meant that everyday kids were dying and suffering, and all you could do was lay there, because there was zero treatment.

In some ways, it was really a nightmare.

HB: In *some* ways?

PZ: Well, what I mean is that, even aside from that, they didn't even have the most primitive sense of social, emotional care for children. You would just lie in a bed. There was no radio, music, or television. There was no mail. And visiting hours were only two hours on Sunday.

It wasn't really two hours, in fact, and not really every Sunday. Because what that meant is that when parents came—on the rare occasions that they actually came—they would wheel your bed against a big window, your parents would be on the other side, and you would talk to them on a phone.

HB: It's like you were an inmate.

PZ: That's right. And then, as soon as there were more than three beds waiting behind you and the next set of parents came in, they would say, "*Okay, finish up. You have to move out.*" At the end of the day, maybe you would get an hour at the most.

This was winter in New York. It was a six-block walk from my home to the subway, a six-block walk from the subway to the hospital, and I was there from late November to April.

During that time, they used to have big storms in New York. My mother was pregnant with my sister Vera. My brother George had polio and braces and there was Dawn as well. So it was clear that my mother couldn't walk those distances; they couldn't afford a taxi, and poor people couldn't afford telephones.

So you wait all week for that magical hour and they don't come, and they don't call. Pretty soon you learn that the key to survival is to be self-reliant. You can't depend on the nurses, you can't depend on the doctors, and you can't even depend on your family.

Essentially, I decided, very consciously, that I was going to survive. I wasn't going to die—it didn't make sense to me to die.

I became very religious. In the morning I would pray to God to make me strong, healthy, and brave, and allow me to survive. And at night, I would pray to the Devil not to take me. I'd say, "*Look, there are a lot of kids. Why me?*"

When it was lights out, at 8 pm or 9 pm, you couldn't sleep because you weren't tired: you hadn't done anything all day. I can still remember that when they turned out the lights and the nurses walked in front of the light, they made shadows—which to me, at that age, was obviously the Devil coming to make his choice.

I would go under the covers and pray to Lucifer not to take me because I was a good kid. I didn't realize until much, much later that what I was doing was practicing self-hypnosis, because then I would wake up and it would be morning. I would never have nightmares; I would just wake up the next morning and realize that I had survived another day.

HB: It's interesting that Lucifer was involved in your life from a very young age.

PZ: I just figured that you double your chances of surviving if you have God on your side as well as the Devil.

HB: Sure, that's very pragmatic. It's like doubling Pascal's Wager.

PZ: Exactly. The other survival tactic I had concerned the nurses. It was clear that they were critical for your social and emotional success, so I learned to give them compliments. They wore masks all the time, so you would tell them what beautiful eyes they had, or beautiful hair, or remark on an earring or something. That meant that they would remember you and you'd get an extra pad of butter or whatever. You'd get preferential treatment.

The most important thing was that they would remember you were sitting on the potty, because they would often forget. You could never get out of bed, so you would have to urinate and defecate in a potty, and sometimes they would forget, or there would be a new nurse on shift who wouldn't know the situation.

To this day, when I talk about my Heroic Imagination Project, one of the most important things I say is, "*Your job is to make other people feel special. Learn their name, use their name, find out something important about them, and give them a justifiable compliment that makes them feel special.*" I started doing that when I was five after I realized that it works.

HB: So this was a conscious decision on your part?

PZ: Absolutely. I would say to myself, "*Everybody around me is dying. I don't want to die. What more can I do besides pray?*" I realized that this was something that I had to do.

And after getting the nurses, the Devil, and God on my side, I figured I had to get the other kids on my side. The only joy that we had was reading hero comic books. Because of contagion, parents couldn't give you any toys or anything. They were poor in any event, but anything that was brought in couldn't go back out. So all we had were these comic books that we shared, devoured, and passed around. I couldn't read at that time. I looked at the pictures and thought they were nice, but I had to ask older kids to help me read the words. I got my mother to give me a pen and paper so I could write down each word. By the time I left the hospital, I could read and write in a primitive way.

The other thing I realized when I was in the hospital was that I needed something to do to relieve the boredom. After you read that Superman comic for the 10th time, what are you going to do? So I would invent games. To the kids who were within earshot, I would say things like, "*Imagine our beds are rafts and we're going down the Nile in search of a white alligator,*" and someone would say, "*Okay, I'll do this,*" and another person would say, "I'll do this".

Essentially, from the age of five on, I began to take a leadership role, not because I wanted to be a leader, but because I was bored out of my mind and I wanted something to do.

It was a way of amusing myself—but then, in the process, I realized the power of the group. If we were all playing some game, somebody would say, "*Hey, I think I see Indians down there,*" and someone else would say, "*Okay, I'll be in charge of killing the Indians,*" and so on.

HB: So you developed a strong sensitivity to group dynamics from a very young age.

PZ: Yes, but group dynamics more in the sense of not being alone. Others were dying around me, alone in their beds. These were resiliency tactics. How do I survive, thrive, and actually enjoy being here?

HB: You were able to have a sense of *enjoyment*?

PZ: Yes, definitely. I was writing things, drawing pictures, playing these games. At some point, I literally stopped thinking about my family because it was just more heartbreak. Even when they *did* come, everybody would be crying the whole time. It was clear that it didn't pay to look forward to that Sunday visit, because if they didn't come the heartbreak was so great. It was better to be surprised if they did come. I think it was a primitive resiliency tactic.

The other sad thing is, whenever you woke up and Billy or Jenny was gone, and you'd ask the nurse, "*Where did Billy go?*" she'd say, "*Billy went home*". And when you'd ask, "*Why didn't he say goodbye?*" she'd say something to the effect of, "*Well, it was in the night and he didn't want to disturb you, but he said to give you his regards*". Then the same thing would happen with another kid.

The interesting thing was that there was a conspiracy of denial between the nurses and the kids. We knew that "going home" meant that you died, but you couldn't say it. Because then you would give up. The problem was, the thing you wanted most in the world was to go home, but you didn't want to go home **that** way; you wanted to go home the other way.

HB: Did you see kids who went home the right way? You must have seen that occasionally. After all, you went home eventually yourself.

PZ: Occasionally kids would go home, yes. In fact, I remember when they told me, "*You're going home*," I wasn't quite sure how to take that. I remember jumping out of the bed and crumbling, because all my muscles had atrophied. I mentioned earlier the failures of this sort of primitive healthcare—there wasn't even a minimal exercise routine. It took me months before I was able to walk again. I had to use a wheelchair when I got home.

Questions for Discussion:

1. To what extent do you think that Phil's early experience of quarantine might have piqued his interest in the "prison experience"?

2. Do you think that Phil would have eventually developed a high level of situational awareness even had he not had his childhood quarantine experience? Are some people simply born with more situational awareness than others?

III. Increasing Awareness
South Bronx rituals and Halloween distinctions

PZ: When I got home, we were even poorer than when I had left. We had to move to an even worse neighbourhood: from Prospect Avenue in the Bronx a few blocks down to 1005 East, 151 St.

For those who don't know, that's the *real* South Bronx: a few blocks further is Southern Blvd. and then a few blocks further is the East River. A lot of people will say, "*I came from a poor neighbourhood in the Bronx,*" and they tell me they lived on Grand Concourse or Fordham Rd. That's nothing. It doesn't get more South Bronx than where we were.

Before I went to the hospital, we used to move every few months because we couldn't pay the bill. My father would plan "midnight adventures." That's when he first started using me to help with the kids. He'd say, "*We're going to move tonight. It's going to be an exciting adventure. We're going to a new place that's even better. There won't be any cockroaches. Tell your brothers and sister about it.*"

I'd wake them up, tell them about this adventure, get them to put on their coats, and we'd move a few blocks away, which meant that we didn't have to pay the back rent and we could start again.

By the time I went to college, we had lived in 31 different places, which meant no stability. We sometimes moved five or six times in a year. I actually still have a list with all the addresses.

Anyway, once I got home from the hospital I was really skinny—in fact, some of my relatives used to call me "bag of bones". We were living in this really bad neighbourhood. And now kids started beating me up. I'm thinking, *Wait a minute. I just got out of the hospital. Why this?*

They'd hit me and run after me hitting me—I think that's how I became good at track—yelling things like, "*Dirty Jew bastard!*"

HB: You're a Jew all of a sudden?

PZ: Well, I was a Sicilian kid, but I looked Jewish to them. These kids were Irish, Italian, Armenian; and because I had blue eyes, a big nose, and I was skinny, in their view, that's what it meant to be a Jew, because there were no other Jews around.

That problem wasn't solved until my mother offered Charlie Glassford, the janitor's son, five cents to take me to church at St. Anselm's on Sunday. Charlie replied that he couldn't take me there because I was a Jew. When my mother told him that we were Catholic, he said, "*Oh, we've been beating him up because we thought he was a Jew.*"

Once they knew I wasn't a Jew, I was allowed to join their gang, which was comprised of kids who were maybe 5 to 10 years old—there was also a teen gang.

To get into the kid gang, there were rituals, primitive, native rituals. You first had to fight the last kid who got into the group. You had to fight until somebody got a bloody nose. Then they would take your sneakers, tie the laces together, throw them up into a tree, and you had to climb up the tree to get them. Then they would put you through a store window at night and you had to steal a box of fruit. You'd also have to steal something from Melvin Semmel's Candy Store: someone would make a diversion, and you'd steal some candy bars that you had to share afterwards. Remember, these were kids who were 5 to 10 years of age—this is what it means to be in a ghetto. Then the last thing you had to do was go under the street in front of the women's negligee stocking store and you had to look up when the women passed. You then had to report what you saw and describe it in great detail.

They were all primitive tasks. It really was like coming of age in a primitive society, like Margaret Mead's *Coming of Age in Samoa*, this was *Coming of Age in the South Bronx*. You had to fight, you had to steal, you had to do a test of agility and strength, you had to undergo a sexual test, and then you were in the group.

It was clear that being *in* the group was better than *not* being in the group. But then I thought, *Why would anyone want to be a follower?* The group leaders would tell you what to do. When we would play stickball in the street, the last kids in had to collect the bats and everything. I said to myself, *"After all this, it doesn't make sense to be a follower."*

So I began to observe the situation. I asked myself, *"What is it that the kids who are leaders do?"* Either they were bigger or they had a buddy who was big. More often than not, they had a buddy who was big, who was a kind of enforcer. Secondly, they were always the ones who would come up with an idea first. Typically they would also change the idea and say, *"No, we're tired of this now. We're going to do something else".* I said to myself, *"Well, I was doing that in the hospital."*

HB: Again, it was a very conscious decision.

PZ: It was very conscious, yes. The entire world is filled with a few leaders and a lot of followers. Obviously—at least from my point of view—it's better to be one of the few leaders than one of the many followers. There are many more perks; and also, especially in this setting, followers were asked to do really awful things, sometimes very dangerous things. Leaders don't do dangerous things. It's just like war: the leaders tell the troops to go into battle while they watch from a safe distance. So I began to practice those kinds of things.

HB: This was another survival strategy.

PZ: Yes, it was a survival strategy.

From that time onwards I started becoming a leader. In elementary or junior high school, you'd have elections for who was going to be class president. I would somehow do the right thing—make a joke, or what have you—and I would end up being the captain or the president.

At Brooklyn College, I was president of my fraternity. I was captain of the track team. I was captain of the softball team in our neighbourhood. I was vice-president of the senior class at James Monroe High School, and so forth.

Then, when I was 15 and a junior in high school, my family moved to North Hollywood, California. My father's entire family—all seven sisters and two brothers—had moved to the Los Angeles area. They said, "*George, we need you to keep our family together.*" So we moved there.

The sad thing was that this was now 1947 and my father was finally doing well with the radio store and everything. We had paid off all our debts, but then we had to spend all of our money on airplane tickets to get there. The job they had lined up for my father didn't materialize, because it was a job as an engineer, and he hadn't even graduated from high school. So he didn't work at all for six months. We were even poorer, and we lived in an even worse place than in the Bronx. It was a devastating experience.

At any event, I was still a good student. I went to North Hollywood High School. It was the most amazing place. You'd get to the school and there's a parking lot filled with motor scooters. And there was the senior parking lot that looked like a scene from *Grease*: Model T Fords with stainless steel motors, and kids polishing them.

On the first day, the bell rings and everybody runs to the auditorium, where there's a student-run assembly. The president of the senior class gets up and says, "*We're going to do* **The Mikado** *this year. Here are the parts. We want all of you to try out.*"

I was so excited to be a part of this. But when I sit down in class all the kids move away from me. The same thing happens in the lunchroom. For six months, I was basically shunned at this new school: no student talked to me, and when I responded to them, they all turned away. I just couldn't understand it. It was such an alien thing to me. I loved this place physically, but I was now just *persona non grata*. The consequence of this was that I developed a psychosomatic breathing problem at night.

HB: You were shunned just because you were the new kid?

PZ: No. That's what I thought too at first, but you're not the new kid forever.

After I made the baseball team, I asked some kid when we were on our way to a game in Van Nuys or Burbank or some place, *"I'm really upset. Why is it that nobody likes me?"*

And he replied, *"It's not that we don't like you. We're afraid of you."*

"What do you mean?" I asked.

And he said, *"We know you're from New York and you're Italian. Everybody thinks you're from the mafia, so we're afraid of you".*

Talk about ignorance or prejudice! I had had no idea: nobody had said anything at all.

But it was too late. Because I had the psychosomatic breathing problem, my family was able to use that as an excuse to go back to New York, rather than say, *"It was a mistake. We failed."*

So we went back to New York. I returned to James Monroe High School, and after three months I was voted "Jimmy Monroe": the most popular boy in the senior class.

One of my classmates was a little Jewish kid named Stanley Milgram, and we talked about this—

HB: Hold on—*really? The* Stanley Milgram? No kidding.

PZ: Stanley Milgram was in my class, yes. He was the one who wrote the little blurbs in the yearbook—*"Phil Zimbardo's tall and thin/with his blue eyes, all the girls he'll win."* That was his blurb for me.

HB: OK—a good psychologist, but not necessarily a great poet.

PZ: Well, he was only a kid. But the point is that the two of us reflected on my experiences and talked about whether it was me or the situation. We agreed it was the situation.

Obviously *I* hadn't changed: I was the same person. When I was at James Monroe, people liked me. Then I went to this other place and people hated me. Then I came back to James Monroe and people loved me again. Not only was I accepted, but I became the most *popular* boy. So we agreed it **had** to be the situation.

Stanley was 15 or 16 at that time and this was not that far from the Holocaust: he was concerned about whether the Holocaust could happen again, and if his family could end up in a concentration camp. I said, *"Stanley, don't be stupid. That was then, this is now. Those are German people. We're not that kind of people."*

And he would say, *"I'll bet* **they** *said the same thing. How do you know what you'd do until you're in that situation?"* That was his big thing as a high school kid. He was a seriously grim kid.

HB: Well, in 1947 he had some reasonably objective, serious reasons to be grim.

PZ: Right. I don't know whether or not any of his family had escaped the Nazis or whether anybody he knew had been in a concentration camp. But we were just kids. We were apolitical—I certainly was—but he was always really serious and really smart. I think he won all the medals at graduation.

HB: These conversations you had with Stanley, about whether it was you or the situation, were these thoughts in your mind as you started to study psychology? Were you already thinking about situational factors?

PZ: Yes, I think that was there. Again, the one positive thing about going to North Hollywood was developing an awareness of how different people behave.

For example, in Hollywood, when it was Halloween, we did something called "trick or treat". I remember that when I was getting ready to go out, my cousin gave me a shopping bag. *"What's this?"* I asked; and he said, *"That's what people put the treats in"*. And I said, *"What do you mean* **'people put treats in'***?"*

In the Bronx, it was a word—"trickertreat"—and then you did a trick. There was no treat. We didn't understand the concept that people would actually *give* you something.

What you would do is, in a big apartment, you'd put pins in all the bells so they would ring until someone came down to pull the pins out, or you'd pile up milk bottles in front of someone's door so that, when they opened their door, they would all fall down. Those were the tricks you did.

HB: It was trick-or-trick, basically.

PZ: Exactly. We didn't understand the components of the word. It wasn't "trick-or-treat"; it was "trickertreat". That was the word.

Halloween in North Hollywood was a dramatic contrast. So I became aware that situations influence not just how you talk, but also how you think.

Another Halloween example: in the Bronx, we used to fill up a nylon stocking with flour and hit people with it, especially girls. It wouldn't hurt, it would just make a big mess. I remember that one of my cousins was outraged when I told him about that. He said, "*How could you do that? I thought you were a nice kid.*"

And I said, "*We all did it.*"

Basically, I became aware of situational norms. What was totally acceptable in one setting was totally repulsive in another.

HB: Years later, when Stanley Milgram came up with his world-famous experiments on obedience and authority figures, were you more sensitive to those ideas because you knew him from a young age? Was it because you were thinking about those sorts of things all along? Or was it simply because it was causing such ripples in the community?

PZ: All of the above. I graduated James Monroe High School in 1950. Then I went to Brooklyn College from 1950 to 1954. In 1954, I went to Yale, while Stanley went to Queens College and worked with Solomon Asch.

When I graduated from Yale, I got my first job at the NYU campus in the Bronx—they had a campus there then. I taught there and also did a graduate course downtown. I started there with John Darley, who, with Bibb Latané, did the key work on the bystander effect, following the murder of Kitty Genovese in New York.

At NYU, I was teaching five semester courses each term plus two courses every summer. I would teach large lecture classes mostly: introductory psychology in the fall, winter, and summer, which came out to 12 courses a year. Then I would moonlight and teach a 13th course. One year I taught at Barnard College. I also went back to Yale to teach an evening Master's course in psychology. And by that time, Stanley had just arrived at Yale and was about to begin his research.

I remember a conversation we had when he was starting. He was a little paranoid because a guy named Arnold Buss had invented an "aggression machine." It was different than Stanley's, but Stanley thought that the idea had been stolen from him, that maybe he had mentioned it in a colloquium or something. So he told me, "*I can't tell you about my research.*" I said that was okay, but that he should definitely keep me in the loop as it developed.

When his research came out, I remember calling him, writing him, seeing him at conventions. In 1971, several weeks after the Stanford Prison Experiment was finished, I gave a talk at the American Psychological Association on something—maybe emotion or something—I don't remember.

And at the end of the talk I said, "*I have to share something with you that's really exciting. I just did this study and I want to take five minutes to explain it to you.*" So I described it, and I might have even had a few slides.

Stanley came over, gave me a hug, and said, "*Oh my God, now you can take all of the ethical heat off my back, because yours is the most unethical study ever done.*" And he was right.

Questions for Discussion:

1. Have you personally experienced a similar scenario to what Phil describes when discussing different Halloween practices, where he accounts for his behaviour by simply saying, "We all did it".

2. Why do you think Phil mentions, off-handedly, The Bystander Effect? What is that and how is it relevant to situational psychology and Phil's future work?

3. Are you familiar with Stanley Milgram's famous experiments on obedience? In what ways do you think that Stanley Milgram and Phil Zimbardo influenced each other's research careers?

IV. Situation Stanford

The 1971 Stanford Prison Study

PZ: So why do that study? What I appreciated most about Stanley's research was that it demonstrated, unequivocally, the power of situations to shape human behaviour—in this case, in a negative way. But my thinking was that it's very rare that somebody in authority will tell you to do something bad and you will do it.

Again, I think Stanley was really thinking of a Hitler, or an Eichmann, or a Mengele. But my sense is that it's really about being part of a group, when the group leader makes suggestions. The group leader doesn't explicitly say, "*Do this*." The group leader puts forward an idea, and suddenly everybody's doing it. I was always more focused on the institution, the system, the context, rather than an individual who creates the situation, and then either you do it or you don't do it.

I was always thinking that if I followed up on those ideas, I would try to do it in *that* type of context. When I came out of the hospital that summer, I went to summer camp and there were camp counsellors who brutalized some of the kids. The Stanford Prison Study could really have been set in a hospital, or a summer camp, or what have you. So for a long time I had the thought to do something like that.

In 1970, when the war in Vietnam escalated to Laos and Cambodia—I was always anti-war, I was not a political person but I was always a pacifist—Ronald Reagan, who was the Governor of California at the time, shut down all California schools, in part so they wouldn't protest.

Stanford had been fairly *laissez-faire* about political stuff—Berkeley was where the activists were—but I got together with some other faculty and organized a Political Action Coordinating Committee at

Stanford to say to students, *"You can't count on Berkeley kids to protest. **You're** going to have to do it."*

The school went on strike in the spring and we organized, through the psychology department, a Political Action Coordinating Committee with something like 2,000 students.

There were some kids who started violent protests—breaking windows and so forth. I said to them, *"That's stupid. How's **that** going to affect the war? Let's think of proactive things you can do against the war. You could get people to sell off their war bonds. You could find out what businesses the Stanford Board of Trustees run that are in support of the war—like Dow Chemical— and expose that. You could get the Stanford Research Institute, which is involved in a lot of secret government issues, to admit to their involvement."*

Suddenly, the students took over. The police had come on the campus, there was a lot of town-gown feuding, and so forth.

HB: Town-gown feuding at **Stanford**? In **Palo Alto**?

PZ: Well, it was for the first time, because when the police came on the campus, they beat up some kids. We'd never had that before. So we organized a kind of police-Stanford diffusion: we had cops have dinner in the dormitories, we had students ride around with the police, and so forth. As a consequence, the chief of police was replaced for not containing the cops. I remember going to the new chief of police, James Zurcher, describing our program and how we wanted to create good community relations.

Later, when I was thinking about doing the Stanford prison study, I went back to him and said, *"We're doing this thing and I'd like your cooperation. I'd like you to help with arresting the prisoners, and I'd like some of your new, rookie cops to be prisoners, so they experience what it's like to be on the other side."* He said, *"That's a great idea. We'll do it."* He later decided not to, and all of the subjects in the experiment ended up being students. But, at that point, I seized the moment.

HB: You were doing the same thing as that five-year-old in the hospital.

PZ: That's right: the same thing. And once he was on my side I told him that a benefit of doing this was that it would allow his cops to see things from the other side. Later he said that he couldn't do it because they couldn't afford to have the cops off-duty for two weeks. But he still agreed to arrange for the police cars to do the arrests.

When my class started up again, I told the kids, "*One of the things I learned from this strike-shortened term that I never appreciated is the amount of energy and creativity students have when they are unleashed, when they aren't simply doing our assignments.*" I said, "*You guys did all of these things and it was very impressive*"—they had a newspaper, they had a rumour-diffusion center.

So I said to them, "*I'm going to divide this social psychology class in half and rename it 'Social Psychology in Action'. I'm going to put my best lectures in the first half of the course, rather than spread them throughout the whole course; and in the second term, **you're** going to take over. Since you have time that I don't, here is a series of topics that I'm interested in that I don't have time to research. Each of you pick a topic, we'll have a graduate student assist you, and you experience it, collect the data, and either you present it in class, or you give it to me and I'll present it.*" Everybody agreed.

One topic was, *Why is it that elderly people, when they go to an old age home, on average, die within the first year, regardless of their health going in?* This was a recent finding that I was curious about.

Again, I was interested in the dynamics of situations—systems and individuals. Another topic concerned prisons: *What happens to somebody when they go to prison for the first time? What is that experience like? How do they adjust to this alien environment?* I asked those who were interested in that topic to sign up, to understand more about the person in the prison.

Curiously, the ones signed up for that group had all been part of a new house plan that was organized around non-violence in response to the student strike. David Jaffe, the undergraduate who was organizing this in my class, came up to me and said that he wanted to do a mock-prison over a weekend, which I said was a great idea.

The day after that weekend, on almost the last day of the term, that group presented in class and described all the things their group had done. They introduced an African-American guy who had just gotten out of prison, Carlo Prescott—one of the students' uncles was a lawyer who had worked with him. He was really eloquent—I knew I should remember that guy because he was both full of rage and very eloquent.

Then the kids started presenting about what they did. Some of them were in tears, saying things like, "*You can't be my friend anymore. You treated me so miserably.*" Then the other would reply, "*No, that wasn't me. I was just playing the guard.*" And the first would say, "*No. The guard is the **real** you.*"

I was stunned. Some of these kids were in tears in front of an audience of 200 people. At the end, I said, "*Wait a minute. We all have to debrief.*" We all went to my lab and I asked them what was happening. It was clear to me that this weekend had been a very powerful experience for these students.

One of the girls had even said to one of the guards, "*If you let me out, I'll let you do anything you want.*" Fortunately, he didn't take advantage of her, or I would have lost my job—but it was at that level.

In discussing this with two of my graduate students who were teaching assistants in that class, Craig Haney and Curtis Banks, it became clear that the problem with this initial experiment was self-selection. Of all the topics available to them, these kids chose prison—they were clearly interested in prison to begin with—and they were all in a house promoting non-violence. I said, "*This is something we should really follow up on. We really need to try to do this correctly, to eliminate this self-selection bias, make random assignments, and so forth.*" They had also had nobody observing the situation, which we clearly needed. That was really the birth of the prison experiment idea.

But I didn't know anything about prison. So at the end of the term, in June, I decided that I would teach a course on the psychology of imprisonment during the summer, and I'd get that guy, Carlo Prescott, to be my co-instructor, because he was obviously out of work and he could tell us about his experience. I also wanted to bring in other ex-cons or prison guards too, which I thought would give me a real sense of what prisons were like, psychologically. The course ended around the first week of August and then we started preparing for the prison study, getting together all the materials, and so forth.

HB: So at this point, you were strongly motivated to look at things from a situational perspective. You're imagining, based upon the other data you got from this weekend experiment—which was self-selected and had methodological problems—that there were very strong feelings that were generated, even with people who were predisposed towards peace. My guess is that you were thinking that this could be a great opportunity to scientifically study the effects of this sort of situational perspective, right?

PZ: Absolutely. But at that point, I didn't recognize the link to Milgram. I was not looking at the experiment as a way of studying, in an institutional setting, what Milgram had been studying on the individual level. That thought didn't enter my mind until the experiment began to unwind.

Then I realized that the key was having some pre-measures, because we really wanted to have good people put in a bad place, so we had to know, from day one, that we had only "good apples".

So we did what Milgram *hadn't* done: we gave a series of personality tests *first* so that we could eliminate anybody with extremes of any personality dimension. All of the subjects were "psychologically normal" and physically healthy.

And then we simply made a random selection and told half of them to either wait at home, wait in the dormitories, or wait on the porch of my secretary Rosanne Saussotte.

Most of the kids had been at summer school at Stanford or Berkeley. That was the reason we did it at that time—we knew that the regular school term typically didn't start until after Labor Day, so everybody had a couple of weeks off.

HB: They weren't all Stanford students though. You said only two of them were, right?

PZ: Right, these were students from all over the country. They had just finished summer school at Stanford or Berkeley. We knew that they needed some money and they had the time off, so there was nothing else competing for their time—they didn't have to study, or what have you.

The key was getting the police to arrest them, so that the police, the authority figures, took away their freedom—because if they had simply come and said, "*Okay, I'm here to begin the study,*" in the same way that they gave up their freedom voluntarily, when the shit hit the fan, they could just as easily have said, "*I quit.*" Well, you can't quit a prison.

In a way, the most powerful thing in the study was the mock arrests by the police, of each of the prisoners separately. They arrested them, read them their rights, took them to the police station, took their fingerprints, took their photo, and put them in a real prison cell in the Palo Alto jail. The police took it very seriously. They blindfolded them and brought them down to our prison, still blindfolded. We stripped them naked, deloused them, put a chain on their legs, and then took off their blindfold. They were standing naked in front of a big mirror with all the guards making fun of them, and they were now ready to be institutionalized.

They put on their uniforms, which was a smock without underpants, to feminize them. They were put in a cell and given a number—they were actually Boy Scout uniform numbers that my secretary had sewn on—and they became a number. That was what started the institutionalization of each of the prisoners.

The study officially began on a Sunday night, August 14th. But it was 1971 and the kids who were playing guards were pacifists, or anti-war activists, or civil rights activists—it's almost like they were out of the chorus of Hair—everybody had long hair. In fact, in their initial interviews we asked them, "*Would you rather be a prisoner or a guard?*" and every, single person said they would rather be a prisoner. They'd say, "*I didn't go to college to become a guard. I can imagine being a prisoner. I can't imagine being a guard.*"

They had real difficulty getting into the role: shift after shift, you can hear it on the tapes. We made a documentary about it called *Quiet Rage: The Stanford Prison Experiment*. The guards would say things like, "*Come on guys, let's take this seriously. No laughing.*"

At the end of the first day, I thought it was over already, because it didn't seem to be going anywhere. I couldn't understand why Jaffe's kids got so crazy. It seemed like nothing to the current subjects at that time.

There were three prisoners in each of the three cells. There were three backup prisoners in case we had to replace any. There were three guards on each of the three shifts, and three backup guards as well. I had an agenda for the things they would be doing—two hours for reading, movie time, and so forth—to make it like a real prison.

I thought, *Nothing is happening here. We'll allow it to go one more day and then, if nothing happens, we'll just end it.*

Then, the next morning, the study was "saved" when the prisoners rebelled—all except one cell. Interestingly, they rebelled because they didn't like to be dehumanized. They didn't like to be called a number. In fact, they ripped the numbers off. Instead of shaving their heads, we had them wear women's nylon stocking caps, just to create a similarity, but they wanted to be individuals.

HB: Did they think this was a game at this point? They knew they had volunteered for an experiment. They were getting paid for this, and so forth. Was this sort of a "mock rebellion" in their minds? They weren't really *that* upset, were they?

PZ: No, they were really upset. What's hard to appreciate is the ethos of the '70s. To be a number was terrible. It was so important to be an individual, to be "me". To have somebody suppress or limit your freedom was the worst thing possible. The '60s and '70s were all about freedom. So the rebellion was serious.

The biggest mistake that they made was beginning to curse the guards to their faces. Somehow, they got a cord—I'm not even sure where they got it from—and they put it around the bars of the cell so the guards couldn't open the door, and they started yelling at the guards, things like, "*You little punk. When I get out, I'm going to kick your ass.*" And the guard would reply, "*When you get out, we'll see.*"

Then the guards came to see me. I usually slept on a foldout couch in my office, and they came to me and asked, "*What are we going to do?*" I replied, "*It's your prison. What do you want to do?*" and they said, "*We need to call in all the other guards.*"

So we called in the standby guards and the guards on the next shift, which meant that there were now 12 guards and 9 prisoners. They said, "*We have to take back our prison from these dangerous prisoners*".

That's where the whole experiment changed. Once they used the semantics, "*These are dangerous prisoners,*" that became the rhetoric. It was no longer an experiment: these were dangerous prisoners who were insulting the guards and embarrassing them. The other guards would say to the morning shift things like, "*What are you, pussies? How could you let this happen?*" They were now personally embarrassed, and the dynamic very suddenly changed. It became us against them.

Prisons are about power. The guards had to demonstrate that they had power and the prisoners had none, because if they gave the prisoners any power, they feared this was going to happen again. So they broke open the doors, dragged the prisoners out, and stripped them naked. There was a lot of physicality—prisoners were cursing and screaming, obviously. In some cases, they even used the cords to tie their hands and drag them into solitary confinement.

It was at that point that the Stanford prison study truly began, as a power dynamic between the guards and the prisoners over who was going to be in charge of this prison.

HB: This was day two?

PZ: This was the morning of day two, yes, the Monday.

I was just an observer. I told them, "*It's your prison.*" The only time I really intervened was when I saw that the guards were ready to hit—they had billy clubs. I said, "*You cannot use physical force. Force is symbolic.*"

Jaffe, the undergraduate who had developed that first weekend study, took on the role of warden. I was the superintendent of the prison, and the two graduate students, Craig Haney and Curtis Banks, were something like my lieutenants. I made an announcement that there was to be no physical force, which became very difficult at times, especially when the prisoners struck back. I said things like, "*It may be that two of you have to hold a prisoner so that you minimize the need for force.*"

At that point, the dynamic changed and became all psychological. Without any training, the guards slipped into psychological humiliation: domination and degradation.

The first thing they did was designate the cell that hadn't rebelled as "the honour cell," announcing, "*They're going to get food and you're not.*" Then they made them sit outside, in front, so the prisoners in the other cells could see. They said, "*They're going to get special privileges. You're not going to get any dinner*", or, "*They're going to get exercise privileges and you're not*". This was the start of the guards beginning to use tactics of degradation and humiliation, which then escalated.

The ringleader of the rebellion—Prisoner #8612, who, in real life, was Doug Korpi—had actually been a student rebel, an anti-war activist, at Berkeley. Right away the guards singled him out as a troublemaker. They put him in solitary confinement and got him to do menial tasks over and over again. He was screaming the whole time.

Then, of course, what the guards would do is play the prisoners against each other: they would say to the other prisoners, "*If he doesn't do this, you don't get a visitor*", or, "*If he keeps doing this, you don't get dinner*", or whatever. So the other prisoners started attacking him. The guards intuitively knew to divide and conquer, a notion which they used throughout the experiment.

Finally, after 36 hours, he had an emotional breakdown—screaming, crying, just out of control. At the time, I was actually at dinner with Carlo Prescott who came down to visit that night. When I came back, I was furious with Craig and Curtis. I thought Doug had psyched them out, that he obviously couldn't have actually had an emotional breakdown, but they said, "*No, he really did. You didn't see it.*" I then listened to the videotape and realized that he surely was having a breakdown. He then became a model of how you get out of the experiment.

There was a Human Subjects Research Committee at Stanford that approved the study. One of the things that I had to agree with was that, if any prisoner said, "*I want to leave the experiment. I want to quit,*" they would have to be released, no explanation needed. That was the magic phrase: you just had to say it. But once they begin to think of it as a prison—you don't say, "*I want to quit the prison.*" I think that notion ties back to the police arrests.

So when a prisoner would say, "I can't stand it any more," I would say, "*Well, write a letter to the parole board.*" So we had a parole board, headed by Carlo Prescott, with secretaries and other people.

The parole board never actually paroled anybody. Of course, the guards wrote reasons why certain prisoners should not be paroled. But then, Korpi's breakdown became the model of how you get out. Each day thereafter, another prisoner would show similar symptoms. So we released a second, a third, a forth, a fifth prisoner.

Clearly I should have ended the study when the second prisoner broke down—I didn't believe the first one. I thought he was faking it. But when the second prisoner broke down the same way, I should have realized. This was just an experiment, and people were having *actual* emotional breakdowns. I had already proved my point. Partly, it was because I had in mind that the experiment was going to run for two weeks, and this seemed awfully early to shut it down.

Craig Haney had to leave on Wednesday for a family emergency, so now it was just Curtis Banks, Jaffe, and I. We only had three people running a study that was going 24/7 and was out of control, with prisoners breaking down every day, parole board hearings, and so forth.

We had built in many of the elements they had in real prisons. We had visiting nights where families could visit. We had parole board hearings. We had a prison chaplain. We had a public defender. We also had to feed the prisoners three meals a day.

It wasn't until the Wednesday that things switched to become sexual degradation. It was curious, in the first few days, Korpi was the only one using obscenities, and the guards were very restrained. But then, on the third day or so, it became more sexual, in various ways: more extreme, more humiliation, more degradation.

It really peaked on Thursday night, when I was physically out of the prison. When I came back, I saw on the video, the guards say, "*Okay, you line up. You're all camels. Some of you are female camels. Some of you are male camels. Males, get behind the females and hump them*"—because camels have a hump, and "hump" is a sexual word. Basically, after just five days, the guards were forcing the prisoners to simulate sodomy. It actually took *longer* in Abu Ghraib for the guards to think of simulated sodomy or simulated fellatio.

I had actually decided to end the study a few hours earlier outside. Had I seen that scene I would have done that separately. But the actual reason I ended the study was due to a now-classic confrontation.

I had decided that before we went into the second week, we needed people who had no personal contact with the study to come down and interview all the prisoners, the guards, and the staff. I was going to get graduate students and young assistant professors to do that. One of the people who was going to do that was a woman who had been my graduate student, who had graduated in June and had just gotten a job at Berkeley. She and I had just started dating. Her name was Christina Maslach. She happened to be in the library and I said, "*Hey, why don't you come down Thursday night and, after the toilet run, let's go to dinner. I've been stuck here for days.*"

She came down, and she saw what I had described as "the ten o'clock toilet run". What that means is that, at ten o'clock at night, when the night shift came on, it was the last time prisoners could actually go to a real toilet. If they didn't urinate or defecate during that time, they were not allowed to go to the toilet until the next morning. That meant that, throughout the night, they had to defecate or urinate in a bucket in the cell, which they hated because it smelled terrible. The guards used this as a last opportunity to demonstrate their power, to demean and degrade the prisoners.

They lined up all the prisoners, they put bags over their heads, and they chained their legs one to the other. The prisoners always had to wear a chain with a lock around one leg, so even when they were sleeping, when they rolled over, it would remind them that they were in a prison. They lined them up like a chain gang, marched them down the yard, outside, up an elevator, even though the toilet was just around the corner. The idea was partly to confuse them—in case anybody tried to escape, they wouldn't really know their way around. This was the last time before going to sleep that the prisoners could be dehumanized by the guards.

I looked at the schedule, and for me it was just, 10:00 p.m.—toilet run; 8 a.m.—breakfast; 11:00 a.m.—parole board hearing; 1:00 p.m.—lunch, and so forth. It was just a series of check marks.

I said, "*Chris, look at that,*" and she began to tear up. I asked her what the matter was and she got really upset. She said, "*I can't look at that!*" I said, "*What's wrong with you?*" I started telling her about the dynamics of human nature and all that, and she just ran out.

At that point, I was stressed to my limit. I was not sleeping regularly. We ran out in front of Jordan Hall—it's now 10:30 at night—and I was yelling at her saying, "*Don't you understand that there are dynamics here that have never been seen or studied before? Most experiments only last one hour, but these people are living and becoming prisoners and guards!*"

She just said, "*It's terrible what you're doing to these boys. They're not prisoners or guards. They're boys in your experiment. They are being mistreated. It's terrible what's happening.*"

I kept trying to reframe it in terms of the dynamics of the situation, but she just said, "*I don't understand how you could see what I just saw and not react the way that I am reacting. I know you*"—she had been a TA of mine—"*You love students. You're a loving teacher. But this situation has changed you. You're not the person that I thought you were.*"

It was just like that kid in Jaffe's experiment who said, "*The guard is the real you.*" Then she said, "*If **this** is the real you, I don't want to have a relationship with you.*" That was the clincher. That was like a slap in the face.

It was now eleven o'clock at night. I said, "*You're right. I will end this study tomorrow. Let's go to dinner and think about how I'm going to shut this down.*"

Over dinner we went over all the steps that I had to go through to shut down the experiment, including that we had to have a full debriefing of all the prisoners and all the guards, and all of them together.

The study ended on Friday, August 20th. I know I wouldn't have psychologically been able to go the full two weeks. I probably would have been able to go over the weekend until maybe Monday or Tuesday, but I'm not sure the prisoners could have endured it.

Questions for Discussion:

1. What do you think would have happened had Christine Maslach not confronted Phil when she did?

2. Do you think that it was appropriate for the Palo Alto police department to be involved at the early stages of the study? Would that be allowed today?

3. Did the Human Subjects Research Committee at Stanford act sufficiently responsibly? If not, what should they have done differently and how might that have impacted the study?

4. Do you agree with Phil that a key aspect of the Stanford Prison Study were the pre-measures to ensure that there were no "bad apples" participating?

V. The Aftermath

Reactions and responses

HB: You mentioned in the preface to *The Lucifer Effect* that you had tried to write that book much earlier, but you weren't able to do it because of the incredible emotional strain of having to relive the experiment. It wasn't until years later that you were able to fully document everything in *The Lucifer Effect*. This idea that you yourself were subjected to these situational effects is an interesting idea that I hadn't fully appreciated.

PZ: Again, what is interesting is that Christina was able to say, "***You have been changed by the situation that you created, not just the prisoners, not just the guards.***" Being part of it, you can't appreciate that—in a funny way, I was "the system": I created this evil situation and I had the power to end it, but because I was embedded in it, I didn't realize that.

For me, I was just doing my job: checking off boxes on a list. That also means that, in that position, I prevented myself from seeing the reality.

She was saying, "*Look what boys are doing to other boys.*" When you step back, the only way you can describe it is "horrific" or "horrendous", but for me at that time it was just a check mark on a list.

As the prisoners were breaking down, I had to determine if it was real or not. I'd take them to student health and we'd try to figure it out. But after the second, third, fourth one...

HB: As you say, *you* were the system. I'd like to explore some of the main lines of analysis you make in *The Lucifer Effect*, but first I'd like to address a personal point of confusion.

As an outsider, as somebody who's not a psychologist, frankly, I find some of this a little bit odd. This is 1971. Your buddy Stanley Milgram has done some other experiments to demonstrate the human capacity for evil—largely motivated, according to what you were saying earlier, by widespread atrocities that everybody was aware of. This was not that long after Nazi Germany and some of the most horrific crimes against humanity the world had ever seen.

The idea that not everybody who was in Germany during that time period was a homicidal maniac, that not everybody who participated in the My Lai Massacre in Vietnam was a homicidal maniac—the idea that people tend to reflect, in their behaviour, the particular constraints and attitudes of specific situations, is not a particularly savoury notion, but it is surely something that must have been in the public consciousness.

Then you do a scientific experiment with guards and prisoners, arbitrarily split, with the students who had no particular predilection for any of this activity or anything like that, and you give a tangible demonstration of the severity of this sort of effect. The particular results you got are a little bit stronger, quicker, and scarier than I would have imagined, but they certainly jibe with everything we've seen in the international scene over the last 50 years. It's not really surprising at some level.

But my sense is that it *was* very controversial—not so much with regard to the whole ethical component—I don't necessarily want to go there, unless you want to—but in terms of the actual scientific results, this finding that particular situations have an enormous effect on people, often considerably changing their behaviour.

So for me, this "Lucifer Effect"—the idea that every human being has this potential within himself or herself—should *not* have been big news. But it seems like it was.

PZ: It *was* news and it's **still** news.

We *all* want to believe that we are the masters of our fate, that our behaviour comes from inner free will, from inner determination.

We all want to *deny* that anything we do is influenced by other people or situational forces.

My mission in life since then has been to present the case for situational power and situational awareness. When I wrote *The Lucifer Effect*, I added the idea that systems are the power behind creating, maintaining, and potentially changing those situations.

But people don't want to buy that. All attempts at "changing", "improving," or "modifying" human behaviour are focused solely on the ***individual*** level.

Therapy, incarceration, sterilization, nutrition, exercise—those things *only* focus on the individual level. There's almost *no* program for changing situations, because it's considered too complicated. Even though we can demonstrate that, for example, PTSD therapy for returning veterans has no effect, we just keep doing it. We know that prisoners get little or no rehabilitation and, in less than three years, 70% are back in prison. Why? Because you put them back in the same situation they were in before. The situation is corrupt, so they end up back in prison.

HB: OK, so I'm afraid I'm just going to repeat myself. It's unsavoury to think that, to some extent, we are the victims of circumstance, or that we are influenced significantly by circumstance, beyond what we might like to believe. But this really isn't news. When Hannah Arendt was talking about Adolf Eichmann and "the banality of evil", this encapsulated the idea that systems are built and they influence individuals.

I'd like to move on to Abu Ghraib in a moment, but I'm still struggling with this whole thing. I mean, surely, *psychologists* must have been aware of this. Do you understand my confusion?

Like most people, I suppose, I like to think that I'm completely in control of my own fate, that I'm impervious to whatever other opinion exists out there. But if you actually study human behaviour, you see this effect all over the place. It's unavoidable—it's distinctly unpalatable, but undeniably omnipresent. So I keep coming back to, *How could your colleagues have missed this?*

PZ: Psychology has been the study of individual behaviour, attitudes, and values, to describe, explain, predict and control the behaviour of individuals. All of personality psychology is about the individual. Developmental psychology is about the individual. Cognitive psychology is about what's happening in the brain of the individual. The new area of neurobiology is the biology of individual thought, feeling, and action. Therapy is the same way—almost all of therapy is the treatment of individual, mental illness. Psychology is really focused on the individual.

It's only social psychology, this sub-area of psychology, that says, *People are often in groups. We have to be aware of group norms and group dynamics.*

HB: When the results of the Stanford Prison Experiment were published and people became aware of a rigorous study that demonstrated this effect, what was the response? Was it something like, *These are extenuating circumstances. This doesn't really apply to us*, or was it more like, *We really do have to rethink this exclusive emphasis on individual behaviour?*

PZ: There was a very mixed reaction. Some people said it was enlightening. It's now come to be regarded as a bookend, with the Milgram study, on abuses of authority. Stanley was concerned with the power of individual authority, whereas I was looking at the power of situational authority, institutional authority, if you will. That covers a lot of ground, and makes us aware that situations influence us much more than we are aware of.

On the other hand, people said, "*You didn't have a control group: you didn't have people who signed up who were not in the study to show that they didn't change over time.*" There was a lot of negative reaction. The study was not enthusiastically accepted. People were not saying, "*Wow, here's a new concept that we should be working into our thinking.*"

Years later, there was a BBC replication of the experiment—it was a farce actually—in which they created a very realistic prison. But there, in the end, the prisoners took over and the guards got emotional and broke down. They had to call in a labour mediator to mediate between the guards and the prisoners because the prisoners were dominating the prison.

Also this: the day after we finished our study, on August 21st, 1971, there was a riot at San Quentin Prison—half an hour from my home in San Francisco—in which George Jackson, an African-American anti-prison activist was killed, along with a number of guards and inmates. Some people say he was set up and murdered.

Three weeks later, at Attica Prison in New York, the prisoners, in sympathy with what they believed to be the murder of George Jackson, went on a hunger strike and then realized that they had new power over the group. Prisoners who used to be in competition—blacks, Hispanics, neo-Nazis—now, together, could take over the prison, and they did. They took over Attica for more than a month.

Because of both of those events, prisons were suddenly hot news on both the West and East Coasts.

There were two Senate Judiciary Committees meeting to discuss prisons, and they invited me to participate. Why me? Because when the San Quentin Prison incident happened, the associate warden—James Park—was on television doing an interview and one of the reporters, who had covered some of the stuff at Stanford for local TV, asked him, *"Does this have anything to do with the dehumanization of prisoners by guards, as was shown in that psychology study?"*

And he basically answered, *"Psychology is bullshit and doesn't relate to this at all."*

Well, somebody heard that and arranged for me to debate him on television in Oakland. Then Larry Goldstein, who was working for *Chronolog*, the forerunner to *60 Minutes*, had heard *that* debate and came to see me and asked if I had any video material, so I showed him what we had.

In October, the Stanford prison study was given nationwide coverage on *Chronolog* in a 15 or 20-minute piece called *Prisoner 819 Did A Bad Thing*. They had documentary footage, an interview with me, and interviews with some of the prisoners and guards. That gave us a lot of instant notoriety.

Then I was asked to testify in San Francisco and Washington D.C. before two Senate Committees on Prisons, along with the warden of San Quentin, the warden of Attica, the head of the Prisoner's Union, and the head of the Guard's Union. I was the only one who didn't know anything about prisons, except that I had taught some cockamamie summer course.

I didn't have the video, so I showed them slides. I began by saying, "*I'd like to begin by showing a few slides of my study so everybody can get a better understanding of it.*" That anchored the Stanford Prison Study as the only thing we all shared, the visual of it. Throughout the whole hearing, people were saying, "*...as we saw in the Stanford prison.*"

The problem with video in those days was that you needed huge video equipment to play it. If I had smaller equipment, I would have done that. That's why I used the slides.

Those Senate Committee hearings plus the piece on *Chronolog* gave the study instant notoriety. Without that, I would have written an article in a journal that only a few professional colleagues would have read, and that would have been it.

At the time, I didn't think it was worthy of a book. I'd thought about it, but I figured it was just a week-long experiment. I had an idea of writing a book, but then I decided not to.

Questions for Discussion:

1. To what extent does recognizing the importance of situational power on our behaviour diminish individual responsibility and accountability?

2. How do you think the large-scale media attention to the Stanford Prison Study affected its scientific reputation and impact?

3. In what ways do Phil's actions during the Senate Committee hearings on prisons clearly demonstrate his ability to influence people's behaviour? To what extent does this experience illustrate the link between visual images and the perception of authority figures?

VI. Outright Denial
Abu Ghraib and the myth of "bad apples"

HB: OK, let me back up for a moment and try to summarize a few things—here's my understanding of some of your main points to be taken away from all of this.

There are different factors that one has to take into account when one looks at behaviour. There's the *individual* sense—and you're not saying the individual sense doesn't exist, or isn't important, or anything like that—but there's also the *situation* in which we find ourselves. And then, at a deeper, meta-level, there are also the *systemic* factors: the power structure that causes that situation to appear in the first place.

So if we're really determined to understand why people behave the way that they do, you have to fully take into account all *three* of these factors.

PZ: That's exactly right.

HB: You're obviously not saying that individuals aren't responsible for their actions—which is a point of view I'm guessing has sometimes been ascribed to you.

PZ: Of course not.

HB: You're just saying that in order to understand the big picture—why people behave the way that they do—one has to recognize all three of these different levels.

PZ: Yes.

HB: OK, so now we move to the infamous scandal at Abu Ghraib Prison, which, as I understand it, is what really prompted you to write *The Lucifer Effect*.

PZ: Yes. Those terrible images of American soldiers and military police degrading prisoners in Abu Ghraib Prison in Iraq were publicly released in 2004.

HB: These images were seen by horrified people all around the world, and there was certainly a loss of moral high ground—to put it mildly—for the United States. And the response from those in power seemed to completely sidestep the structural factors that we've been talking about.

Instead they said, *"There are a few bad apples"*. The focus was *entirely* on the individuals involved—*"It's not the fault of the system. It's not the fault of the circumstances that were established by that system."* It was a complete denial of the behavioural framework that we were just discussing. I don't want to keep bringing up Nazi Germany, but it's a pretty obvious example of depredations on an enormously large scale.

I'm guessing that this is troubling for you for two reasons: one, because it is obviously a distortion of reality as you perceive it; and two, to some extent, it's a denial of responsibility.

It's a denial of responsibility, because if you take into account all three of these factors we just spoke about, then you have to admit, *"Our system, our structure screwed up. We didn't make sure that these people received proper training, that they were able to recognize the situation that they were in, what the power structure was, and so forth."*

And then you personally became involved in all of this. You were called as an expert witness for the defense…

PZ: Yes, that's a really good analysis. Abu Ghraib was a replay of the Stanford prison study on steroids—exponentially worse.

Things went on 12 hours every night for three months, and the few pictures that were shown publicly—a dozen pictures or so—were nowhere near the worst. I actually have access to a thousand of these images, which are truly horrendous: every different kind of degradation you can imagine, performed by American men and women, military police soldiers, on Iraqi prisoners in their charge, night after night for three months.

One of the first questions you have to ask is, *How could that happen for **three months**?* When you see the pictures, you assume it must have taken place on just one night. So right away, that means that somebody was not minding the store, that there was a systemic flaw.

What I wanted to say before—and you made this very explicit—is that once Cheney, Rumsfeld, and General Myers, Head of the Joint Chiefs of Staff, said, *"This is the work of a few bad apples—renegade, rogue soldiers,"* what that really says is, *"Blame it only on the individuals."*

General Myers actually said, *"There is no evidence that it's anything **but** those individuals. Our army, our training is above that. There is no other evidence of such a thing happening anywhere else."*

It turns out that was a lie: at the same time Abu Ghraib was happening, the same sorts of things were happening at a number of other prisons.

They said that these were not real soldiers because all the military police were army reserve, which means they don't get the same training. Well, I identified an airbase where everybody is a trained airman and they were beating up prisoners with metal softball bats, for stress release. This is documented. Many of them took pictures, and when Abu Ghraib came to light, they made statements saying, *"We destroyed our pictures."*

So the generals effectively say, *"Don't blame the system. Blame the individual. If you blame the system, then we are all involved."*

I should also say that I think they *really believed* that. I think they really believed that, when somebody does something bad, it's from within them, the evil is coming out, and it would come out whether they were in this situation or another one, whether the system did anything to prevent it or not.

But you're absolutely right. My analysis is that we have to know what each individual brings into a situation. Personality *does* make a difference in some cases, as does your background and training; but that's just the *start* of the analysis.

You bring these things *to* the situation. So let's look at this particular situation. The abuses only took place during the night shift. Not one abuse occurred during the day shift. That's a situational variable.

Ivan "Chip" Frederick was the sergeant who was in charge of the night shift. He had been in the army reserve, the National Guard. He was an honoured soldier—he had nine medals and awards—he was an outstanding patriot: he used to take pictures holding the American flag and he would give the flag to people as a gift. He went to Abu Ghraib and had visions of making it a better place. And, in a very short time, he was doing these terrible things that you saw in these images.

One of the motivations for evil is boredom. The worst abuses in the Stanford prison study were at night. The guards would come in, and they had eight hours to kill. The prisoners were sleeping, they had nothing to do, so they would wake them up and play with them.

At Abu Ghraib, Fredrick and the other guards worked 12-hour shifts, from 4 pm to 4 am. Then, at 4 am at the end of the shift, he went to sleep in a prison cell in a different part of the prison, because the prison was always under bombardment. He never left the prison, so he was situationally-bound.

You're bored, you've got nothing to do, and somebody says, "*Hey, I've got a good idea: why don't we strip the prisoners naked and pile them up in a pyramid, and we'll all take pictures of it*".

Once you do that, you can't do it again, because that's boring. So they say, "*Now, let's line them up and have a masturbation contest*", or, "*Now, let's line them up and have them simulate fellatio*". Now they are competing for who can come up with the most interesting idea. Essentially, the prisoners are their playthings.

The worst guard in the Stanford prison study was a man whom the prisoners referred to as John Wayne. He was interviewed shortly after Abu Ghraib and said, "*With enough time, we could have gotten there. We could have done what they did at Abu Ghraib.*"

They actually got there sooner. He said, "*We were just getting our jollies off. No big deal.*" Then he said, "*We were like puppeteers and they were our puppets.*" That's the ultimate dehumanization.

Who were like puppets? Other *students*, who, by a flip of a coin, could have been in the exact opposite situation. This is how an individual immersed in that situation begins to get a distorted sense of reality.

HB: The fact that these sorts of abuses seem to be so incredibly widespread is very revealing too, to my eyes. Looking at it from the outside, one is tempted to say, "*Well, these are clearly sick people. These people are statistically significant in terms of how they were chosen.*"

But what you demonstrated in the Stanford prison experiment, and what you seem to see over and over again, is that these sorts of things happen to normal people with no obvious sign of pathology.

PZ: I'd say super-normal. I interviewed Chip Fredrick. He actually came to my home. I spent the day with him and his wife. We had meals together. He was the most normal guy imaginable. I would have no hesitation to let him take care of my kids. But he gave in to the power of the situation.

Once somebody started saying, "*Let's take pictures,*" they lost all sense of humanity: the prisoners they were humiliating and degrading were simply objects of enjoyment.

During his trial, he said, "*I'm guilty as charged.*" It was a military trial with just a single military judge. I said, "*Your honour, I believe Chip Fredrick is guilty as charged. He says so himself, and he is responsible for his actions, and anybody in those pictures is guilty as shown. However, the severity of his sentence should be mitigated by the fact that, I believe, he would never have done any of the things he did were he not put in that situation. None of the guards on the day shift did anything negative at all, because on the day shift there were senior officers present all the time. On the night shift, in three months, not a single senior officer went down there.*"

That was the most extreme situational difference. Why didn't they go down? When the insurgency broke out, the FBI, CIA, and the American military establishment were caught totally unaware, because Bush had already declared, "Mission accomplished." Then, what they did was start arresting all the boys and men around any explosion, putting them in Abu Ghraib and interrogating them. And they got nothing, because most of them had no information to give.

Most analysts I spoke to said that, at most, 2% of all the prisoners in Abu Ghraib had any "actionable intelligence." But *which* 2%? They were interrogating them and getting nothing. The pressure was coming down from Bush and all the military leaders at the top.

Suddenly, military intelligence goes to the military police heads and says, "*Your guys have to take the gloves off. We need actionable intelligence. We need your guards to prepare the prisoners so that when we interview them, they will spill the beans.*" Essentially they were saying, "*Do whatever you have to do.*"

HB: This is that systemic aspect. You have a huge systemic force that's acting on these situations from above and framing the situations.

PZ: Right. They're creating a new situation by effectively saying, "*Do whatever you have to do. We don't care.*" In fact, not only, "*We don't care*," but, "*We're never going to notice*." Had the guards not taken the pictures, they could have done worse things. Nobody would have noticed. Nobody would have cared.

HB: Maybe they did somewhere else, or under some other circumstances.

PZ: That's right. Whoever sold those pictures to the media probably made a lot of money, and that brought to light this terrible thing that was happening. But the military police and military intelligence originally said, "*We don't want to know. We don't care. All we want to know is that, when we interrogate somebody, they're going to spill the beans.*"

Questions for Discussion:

1. Do you think that these sorts of abuses happen with higher frequency in an environment where photographs can be taken? If so, why do you think that is? What role might the notion of "visual proof" play in the social dynamics of competition and one-upmanship?

2. To what extent is a rigidly hierarchical environment that systemically reinforces the importance of "following orders" compatible with a belief in individual moral responsibility?

VII. Learning Our Lessons?

Towards a deeper level of awareness

HB: I'd like to go beyond the politics—

PZ: Me too.

HB: Because it seems to me that no matter what sorts of conflicts or situations we're in—whether it's war or any sort of systemic situation—we have to recognize that there is a predisposition for these things to happen.

I'd like to discuss how we can go forwards and have some sort of positive effect. What I'd like to hear—and I'm guessing this is not what you're going to tell me—is that there are psychologists working within, say, the US military, or within similar structures, that can recognize some of these things and say, "*Hold on a minute.*"

I'm not expecting the government of the United States is going to take responsibility for this sort of thing. I think it's very clear that they are going to pin it on a few bad apples—it's obviously far easier for them to do that.

But have you noticed any changes anywhere in the system, writ large?

PZ: Larry James, a lieutenant colonel and psychologist colleague of mine, was working in the Pentagon. After Abu Ghraib was exposed, he was sent there by his superiors to develop procedures to prevent it from happening again. He actually invited me to go with him, and I was tempted to go, but it was in the middle of the war and it just seemed too dangerous.

He actually developed PTSD and wrote a book about his experiences (*Fixing Hell: An Army Psychologist Confronts Abu Ghraib*). Essentially what he says is, "*The only way to prevent recurrence of these kinds of horrific actions is to have clear oversight, explicit, public, rules of procedure that everybody recognizes, to have senior officers in charge who are responsible for the actions of their subordinates, and for any subordinate to know that violation of any of these rules will be costly.*"

When he went to Abu Ghraib, he saw that, even after all the notoriety, all the trials, things were still not under control. He essentially imposed this ruling from the top down.

Guards in prisons, everywhere in the world, can have unlimited power. That has to be contained by the system. And that power obviously has to be mitigated not only by moral, humanitarian concerns, but also by concerns for public image. The things you can't do and the things you're not allowed to do have to be made explicit, along with the consequences.

It's possible for the system to recognize that it has made a mistake and try to rectify that in some way.

HB: This is obviously important, but these are programmatic prescriptions that don't explicitly mention what we talked about before—that there are three levels of factors, and so forth—it seems to me that they're more just means to an end to try to minimize the likelihood of things getting out of control.

PZ: The idea is that you can prevent a recurrence by having situational checks, by having a list of dos and don'ts. At least it's something.

Is *The Lucifer Effect* being taught at West Point or Annapolis? I don't know. But surely our next generation of military leaders should buy in to this three-part analysis. You want to minimize the focus on the individual.

Earlier you mentioned Nazi Germany—to this day, people still say it's all about Hitler, but if you read any of that history, the most obvious thing is that Hitler's power stemmed from establishing systemic control. Once you gain control over education, business, communication, media, propaganda, housing, and all the rest, he's irrelevant. Once those things are in place, if any of the attempts to kill Hitler had succeeded, nothing would have changed.

HB: I'd like to move on to the Heroic Imagination Project, but before I do, I have a more personal question. You've spent a lot of time looking at how people—yourself included—can do remarkably bad things, how normal, otherwise non-psychopathic individuals are capable of doing these horrifically bad things.

You play with the idea of Lucifer, this notion that has been recognized by people over the centuries, this notion that each human being has the capacity for good and for evil.

You've developed this analytical framework that we spoke about earlier, about the importance of looking at all 3 aspects of things: the individual, the situational and the systemic. It all sounds very reasonable to me, though perhaps a little depressing—although as someone with a scientific background, I appreciate that's besides the point: if that's the way it is, then that's the way it is.

But my question is this, *Do you have trouble sleeping at night?* I have to tell you, when I was reading your book, I had to skim it. I personally can't even handle the stuff about puppies being shocked. But you had to rigorously go through all this horrible material. I'm guessing that had to be extremely difficult for you on a human level.

PZ: Writing *The Lucifer Effect* took two years. It was horrific. I'm still old fashioned—I don't have everything on my computer—so I had crates of all these horrible events: an Abu Ghraib crate, a Stanford prison study crate, a crate of massacres, and so forth. It was extremely difficult to go through all of that.

I should say two things, though.

The first is—again, going back to the Bronx, back to when I was six years old—my interest in evil developed because I had friends who I knew were good kids but who did really bad things, in part because there were older guys who gave them money for selling drugs, for taking drugs, for stealing, for girls to sell their bodies, and so on. I could never understand why they gave in, because I had other friends who didn't do it, and I didn't do it either. Even as a kid I was wondering, *Why is it that some kids get seduced to do bad things, whereas other kids can resist?*

My simple analysis was that it had to do with having a good mother, a tough mother, who said, *"This is wrong. This is right,"* or, *"Don't play with **those** kids,"*—a mother who, if you brought home money, would ask, *"Where did this money come from?"* and if you couldn't explain, she'd tell you to give it back, or she'd take it away from you.

The point is that I began with the assumption that they were good kids, because I knew that when they were with me, they were good kids—I wasn't even thinking about situational effects at this point—but when some other guy was around, with some money or drugs, they became bad kids. Just putting people into boxes of "good apples" and "bad apples" is very superficial.

And everything I had seen about Abu Ghraib up to that point was like that—so superficial. There were 12 or 13 investigative reports, some 200 or 300 pages long, and I read every one in detail. I told myself that I *had* to bring all of this together, but it only made sense in context of the Stanford Prison Study. The problem was that I couldn't remember all of that.

So what I did was to sit down with two students of mine from Stanford and transcribe the 12 hours of original videotapes that I had fortunately transferred to CDs. We looked at each day of the video, took notes, and had discussions about it. Then we wrote up a typescript of exactly what was said by each one of the guards and prisoners.

I then realized that this was the way I had to present the Stanford prison study. I couldn't present it as historical reconstruction, which is boring. I had to present it in present tense, because that's the way to really recapture and relive it.

Essentially, I was able to present a description of the prison study, presented almost day by day with no psychological terms for eight or nine chapters. Then, finally, in chapter 10 or so, I could ask, *"What does all this mean?"* before moving to, *"Let's look at dehumanization tendencies, de-individuation,"* and so forth.

I think that was the only way to suck readers in, by having an interesting narrative that they could understand. Then after a description of the Stanford Prison Study I said, *"This is one study. How am I able to make these generalizations?"* and I had two chapters that revisited all the other studies, like Milgram's. Finally, once I laid out the background and the analytical tools, I could say, *"Now we are ready to go to Abu Ghraib."*

HB: But that must have taken its toll, personally.

PZ: It was the hardest thing I've ever done. It was horrible. It was two years of the most difficult writing I've ever done. Each night I would go to bed thinking, *Oh my God!* and then the next morning I'd start up again and have to look over what I had written the previous day, and it would get worse and worse.

Questions for Discussion:

1. How likely do you think it is that future Abu Ghraib-like revelations will occur? And if they don't, is that a sign that governments are better at preventing future Abu Ghraib-like abuses from happening or merely better at making sure that there are no leaks?

2. Should **The Lucifer Effect** *and other such books, like Larry James' memoir, be required reading at West Point and other military training facilities in the United States and elsewhere?*

3. What role could/should the media play in reducing the likelihood of human-rights abuses like what happened at Abu Ghraib?

VIII. The Flip Side
The Heroic Imagination Project

PZ: That's why, when I finished the Abu Ghraib chapter, I said to myself, "*Nobody is going to read this. It's so horrific. I need to come up into the sunshine, and the reader does too.*"

I realized I had to do two things: I needed to say, "*It's **not** everybody, all the time. Some people are able to resist these negative influences. I was able to do it as a kid in the Bronx, but I gave in to it in the prison study, because I let the role take over for me.*"

So I made the first part of the next chapter, basically, "Dr. Z's advice on how to resist the negative power of the situation". Then I started thinking about how, when everybody is going the wrong way, the person who *doesn't* go that way can be thought of as a hero.

Curiously, I had never thought much about heroes. Clearly Christina Maslach was a hero. I should have started studying heroes at that point. As a kid, I read comic books about heroes. But somehow, I never focused on heroes.

HB: I think it's interesting that, through the Heroic Imagination Project, you are, at least to some extent, redefining the concept of "hero". I think we all have these cardboard cutout views of what a hero is, but you're exploring this idea of the heroic potential within all of us as a counterpoint to the evil potential within all of us.

PZ: That's exactly right. As a skinny, frail kid growing up with superhero comic books, I thought, *These characters are fun and amazing, but **I** could never be that.* But as a little kid, I had what they *didn't* have: brains. They were the creation of some cartoonist, but I was creating, in Willard Parker Hospital, situations for other kids that were, maybe not as fantastic, but more interesting than just reading comic books. I could lure the kids away from the comic books and get them to play the game of the white alligator, for example.

HB: Meanwhile, even *you*, as you've repeatedly pointed out, went towards the dark side during the Stanford Prison Experiment.

PZ: Very much so. I still feel guilty about it. I allowed evil to exist. In the breakdown of every one of those kids, I am as responsible as any of the guards—perhaps even more so—because I saw what was happening and didn't stop it.

HB: But for me, as an outsider, that's even more emphatic proof of some of the points that you're making. I mean, if you—an adult with a psychological background who is very sensitive to these ideas—if even *you*, under those circumstances, could be prey to this phenomenon, then that further illustrates its potential universality. It's not ironclad proof, of course, but it's perhaps another demonstration.

PZ: Right. Think about all the smart people that Bernie Madoff deceived. Every conman, every hustler, is able to manipulate people's view of the situation to get them to think differently about taking a risk—convincing them, for example, that it's not actually a risk at all.

What we haven't talked about is the semantic distortion of reality. For most people who are engaged in evil deeds, one of the things they learn is the power of words to create images that people buy into. There's a whole world of people who are fraud-mongers, fraud-makers, and we don't have much training for and awareness of that kind of evil.

HB: But I'd like to focus now in going the other way: not just examining the potentialities within all of us to do something very unpalatable, but also thinking about how we might be able to go to the other side, as it were, and become whistleblowers.

You talk about the whistleblower at Abu Ghraib and what he had to deal with afterwards, which was pretty horrific.

PZ: That's right. The guy who stopped the abuse at Abu Ghraib was a young, army reservist—private Joe Darby—the most ordinary guy in the world. He was in his early 20s. His buddy showed him a CD with thousands of images. He reported afterwards that, at first, he thought it was funny. He had never seen anything like it before. But as he looked through more and more of the pictures, he became horrified. He said, *"We're supposed to be bringing freedom and dignity to these people, and we're humiliating them."*

The heroic deed he did was to take the CD, add a little note and put it in the mailbox of a senior investigating officer. He came back the next day and it was still there and he realized that the guy could just throw it away and that would be the end of that, because it was the only copy. So he took it out and went to the senior investigating officer personally and said, *"Sir, I'd like to share this with you."*

That was the really heroic thing: to realize that this was the only evidence he had, which could be easily destroyed and might well have been. When he handed it to him in person there were several weeks of debate regarding what they should do about it—it was almost like the debate about what they were going to do with *The Pentagon Papers*. When Daniel Ellsburg gave *The Pentagon Papers* to the *New York Times*, they didn't publish them right away. The editors spent weeks debating what they should do.

So they debated, and finally concluded, *"We have to do this."* Darby knew that his buddies were going to get dishonourably discharged, no question. He knew it would be a slap in the face for the Bush administration and for the military, but he felt that he had to do it anyway.

In his hometown newspaper, there was a huge headline, *Darby the Snitch*. He comes from a very conservative, rural town. He had to be put in protective custody for three years, together with his mother and his wife. Fortunately, when this blew over and the trials were finished, he was given a hero's honour at the Kennedy Center.

He typifies what I call the everyday hero, an ordinary person who has no special training and no particular social background, but in a specific situation, says, *"Something is wrong and somebody has to* correct it. Somebody has to do the right thing when people are doing nothing, or the wrong thing. I will stand up, speak out, and take action."

When I thought about that I said to myself, "*I should give up evil, give up dining in Hell, and begin to promote that notion that all of us have the potential, with training and guidance, to do the right thing, the heroic thing.*"

HB: I think an important point to make, or at least one that I take from all of this, is that it would be a mistake to say that even this individual, even Joe Darby, is cut from a different cloth and, therefore, cannot commit evil deeds.

Clearly what he did was very impressive—he reacted in a heroic way, as you've said, under very difficult circumstances—but it's possible that on a subsequent occasion, under different circumstances, he might do something just as evil.

PZ: Yes. His buddy was Corporal Graner, who was one of the ring leaders of many of the abuses. Again, if he was on the night shift in the yard, he would have been sucked in in a second. There's no question about that in my mind.

We're not saying that he's on a higher moral plane. He was literally *out* of the situation, just looking at the images, not in the situation where somebody said, "*Take the picture,*" or "*Why didn't you come in this picture with us?*" But if he was there, I'm sure he would have gotten in too, just as if it were a family picture.

The whole idea I had was that heroism really starts in the human imagination—that is, to think of yourself as having an inner hero. All of us as kids wanted to do good. We all wanted to do the right thing. Maybe not the Superman thing, the superhuman thing, but the *right* thing: to help kids who are not doing well, to help our parents, and so forth. It's really about thinking of yourself as an everyday hero: I can do little things that are on the path of heroism.

Essentially, it's saying, "*Be situationally aware.*" In the Bronx, we say "street savvy." Step one is to look around and see what's happening. What's wrong? What's right? What are people doing that they shouldn't be doing? Who needs help? Who needs help but doesn't know how to ask for it? What is it that you *could* do, that's easy for you to do, and you have the skill to do? What can you do that's a wise action, a simple action?

When you analyze a situation and it looks dangerous, what do you do? You call the police, you call 9-1-1, you call for help, you call the fire department. You don't do it yourself. You tell people, *"That's the exit there, not the one you came in from where everybody's getting crushed,"* when they run out of the rock-concert fire. You say, *"Follow me."* There are things you can do—ordinary, simple things.

The other thing that I began thinking about is that we really want to prepare people for that moment in time when the big hero opportunity comes. It's not going to come to many people, and it will probably only come once in a lifetime. So *when* it comes, you want to take advantage of it, because otherwise, for the rest of your life, you'll think to yourself that you could have done the right thing but you didn't act.

How do you get people to practice what I call "the social habits of heroism"? How do you do a little thing everyday so that when the big challenge comes it's only a slightly bigger step? I began to think about what activities we could get people to do, thinking about it as "heroes in training"—we're all of us heroes in training: training for the opportunity when we might be in Joe Darby's position, or Wesley Autrey's position—the African-American man in New York who jumped on a subway track to save someone.

When I got to writing chapter 16 of *The Lucifer Effect,* the obvious first thing I did was a literature search. And the most amazing thing was that there's almost no research on heroism. I realized that the words "hero" and "heroism" *do not exist* in the lexicon of psychology. It's not in any introductory psych textbooks, including my own. It's not a concept that is talked about.

HB: Why do you think that is?

PZ: I have no idea. There's not a body of research. The only related research concerns the Holocaust—interviews with Holocaust survivors 20 or 30 years later. In fact, nobody really studied the Holocaust until Hannah Arendt. She really popularized what happened there.

The idea is to begin with this notion of the superhero, then to look at these people who perform very dramatic actions, and then to look at people who do ordinary activities.

There's something called the positive psychology movement, started by Marty Seligman, a friend of mine at the University of Pennsylvania. He wrote a book with Christopher Peterson called *Character Strengths and Virtues*. The words "heroism" and "hero" don't appear in the entire 800 pages or so of that book. When I asked him about it he said, "*It's not a virtue, it's an action. Empathy is a virtue. Compassion is a virtue.*" My argument is that empathy and compassion without action are *worthless*. They make you feel good, but that's about it.

A few years ago the Dalai Lama came to Stanford and I was privileged to have a public discourse with him. I began by asking him, "*Your Holiness, with all due respect, in a world filled with evil, is compassion alone enough? Does compassion not have to be socially engaged? Doesn't it have to be transformed into heroic action? Does it change anything otherwise?*"

HB: What was his response?

PZ: He hemmed and he hawed. Then his translator asked me to give some examples.

HB: Give some *examples*? It's a fairly easy question to understand.

PZ: Well, he doesn't want to understand it, because the Dalai Lama believes that, at some point, everybody in the world will be compassionate and then, by definition, evil will cease to exist.

That's *never* going to happen. The same sort of hustling that was happening in the Bronx when I was a kid is still going on. Those guys are not going to go to meditation training. They're not going to become compassionate.

HB: Moreover, the situations need to change, according to your thesis. It's not as if we are either good or evil and we can just flick a switch and be one way or the other.

PZ: That's right. In the end, the Dalai Lama said, "*Maybe.*"

Compassion is now a big area of study. At Stanford, I'm on the board of directors for *The Center for Compassion and Altruism Research and Education*. There are compassion contracts, compassionate cities—compassion simply means an awareness of other people's suffering. Empathy is feeling the suffering.

But unless you take *action*, you just feel good; you don't change anything. If I'm lying there bleeding, I don't want you to come over and say, "*I feel your suffering.*" I want you to pick me up and get me the hell out of there—stop the bleeding, or get somebody who can. It seems so obvious that heroic action is the essential behaviour that should be coupled with empathy and compassion.

Questions for Discussion:

1. Do you agree with Phil that, had Joe Darby been on the night shift, he "would have been sucked in in a second?"

2. Does Phil's personal experience with "the dark side" during the Stanford Prison Study give him more, or less, credibility when discussing these issues?

3. What are your first impressions when you hear the word "hero"? Do you feel that the notion of "being a hero" is something that is accessible to everyone? In what ways is the word fitting? In what ways is it not fitting?

4. Do you agree with Phil's analysis of the Dalai Lama's position?

IX. Spreading The Word
Cultivate heroes, and broader understanding

HB: To me, the Heroic Imagination Project seems like a really interesting and important idea where you're focusing on the positive potential of the human condition: a way to try to prime people towards heroic activity or heroic action such that they can take that initiative when the time comes, and so forth.

But let me play devil's advocate for a moment, as it were. Let's suppose I'm some wealthy philanthropist who's interested in contributing more funding to your project (I'm not, sadly, I should tell you straight off). So I might well say, *"This is all very well and good, Phil, but what are your specific measurables? How can we see that what you're suggesting is actually going to have an impact?"*

PZ: Measurables are critical. On our website, we list activities you can do every day. It's about building the social habits of heroism. What are the little things you can do every day? Deeds of kindness, deeds of caring, deeds of helping.

Make somebody feel special: get to know their name, use their name, give justifiable compliments. There's a whole range of things you can do, but the anchor is knowledge.

What I have developed with my HIP team in San Francisco is a new, revolutionary educational program designed for high schools and colleges. Essentially, it takes the best of social psychology domains and puts that in a whole new format based around videos.

The teachers don't lecture. Teachers are more like coaches. They present the video and ask questions. Kids share their view with a partner, and if one of them wants to share it with the class, she can.

We have different lessons—incorporating fundamental social psychological concepts such as the bystander effect and growth mindsets and bias reduction—that we've tested both in minority schools in Oakland and privileged schools in Palo Alto to show that they work. Kids like it. Teachers like it. They really get engaged.

Getting back to your question, one specific measure is, *What do they remember of this experience? And how excited are they for more of these lessons?*

Lessons integrate videos and classroom discussion. Take the Bystander Effect. After watching a video about it there would be many associated discussion questions that the class could engage in, like, *"Think of a time when somebody was in need and you helped. Write it down. Who was the person? What was the situation? How did it make you feel?"*

Then the teacher might say, *"OK, now let's reverse the situation. When was a time that somebody needed help and you didn't help? Write down all the details. How did it make you feel? Share it with your partner. Now, make a commitment that, when you're in that situation again, you will take action."*

HB: Has this been well received by teachers? Is it catching on?

PZ: It is. We are getting engagement throughout the US and around the world. I presented some ideas to the Polish Minister of Education of Poland recently.

HB: Poland?

PZ: As it happens, I'm bigger in Poland than in the United States. There's a Polish scientific publisher, PWN, that publishes all my textbooks. Everything I write, they publish within a year. *Psychology and Life*, which is the oldest, continuously selling textbook in all of psychology—it's in its 20th edition—is the only book used in every Polish college.

Whenever I check into a hotel in Poland, the receptionist pulls out the book and asks me to sign it. The kid carrying my luggage will come back up and ask me to sign his book too.

Anyway, I described what we were doing to the Minister of Education. We had everything translated into Polish. She said, "*We need this sort of thing, because teachers hate school, kids hate school, and parents hate school.*" This is the Minister of Education talking…

She has a big problem on her hands if nobody likes school. I said to her, "*We think kids will love this.*" Of course, we're going to have pre- and post-measures.

What they learn is not just the content; it's a change in attitude and values. The key is behavioural intention. There's a lot of research that shows that, if people explicitly posit, *I intend to do X*, when the opportunity presents itself, they are more likely to do it than people who have not previously formulated that intention. It's a form of psychological readiness. So we would measure that before they take the course and then again afterwards.

We are developing programs in Hungary, Indonesia, Italy, the Czech Republic and other places throughout the world. We're also working with companies to help them better appreciate important issues like social bias and the bystander effect.

HB: Another thing I was thinking about as I was reading your book is the role of the media, and the sensitivity to understanding what both a "hero" and a "villain" is and could be.

The "bad apples" view—to get back to Abu Ghraib—seemed to me to be swallowed very easily, by pretty much everyone. There was no questioning. Nobody seemed to be saying, "*Wait a minute. Didn't Phil Zimbardo come up with some evidence some time ago which suggests that this isn't the whole story?*" Once you say "bad apples," you're slamming the door on any further investigations to systemic issues.

What needs to be done, and how can we do that? How can we educate the media to be more critical, to understand the nature of both evil and heroic acts? This naturally has huge public policy implications as well.

PZ: Absolutely. I've always been sensitive to the importance of media and tried to work with them. I've been on *The Daily Show*, *The Colbert Report*, *20/20*, *That's Impossible* and many more. The media is really the link between experts and the general public.

I've always believed that, in trying to give my psychology away to the public, I have to give it away to the media and *they* have to sell it to the public. That is, I have to work in various ways with media, with reporters, with journalists, to reframe my work in ways that are accessible, easy to understand, and not too academic.

HB: I don't know the answer to this, but is there anything that can be done more generally? After all, what you seem to be saying is exactly what I would expect someone in your position to say, namely, *"I have to get out there to tell my story, taking every opportunity I can to package information in a way that is accessible to people."*

But—without any disrespect intended—that doesn't actually seem to be what's really happening. I'm frustrated because I see the same stuff on television. It's always the same simplistic positioning and knee-jerk scapegoating. Of course the offenders at Abu Ghraib were responsible for what they did; but it's unreasonable, at least to me, to think that they were the *only* ones with any responsibility, to treat those events like they somehow happened in a vacuum.

We talked about Abu Ghraib. We don't have time to go into Guantanamo Bay, but you mentioned, in your book, how the same sorts of things went on there. The very fact that President Obama vowed that one of his first actions after taking office would be to shut it down, and it's still open—that speaks volumes, in my view, in terms of what needs to be done with regards to making genuine advance.

PZ: Yes. My answer was only a partial one. I've described what I've tried to do personally. I'm doing the best I can, but it's not enough.

Maybe the American Psychological Association or the Association for Psychological Science have to have special media sessions at conventions, sessions only for the media about how to better inform people of some of these basic truths in psychology. I'm not sure.

The evening news always starts with the negatives—"if it bleeds, it leads"—and any good story is always tucked in at the end, like somebody saving a cat, or a dog doing a heroic deed.

I agree with you entirely. The media controls access to all ideas for the general public. We need to figure out how to educate the media in ways that are interesting for them. Maybe psychologists have to be on the staff of various media schools, like UCLA, USC, or Northwestern, places that have media programs? I haven't done any of that because nobody's asked me, and I haven't pushed in that direction, but there's no question in my mind that it's really critical.

Many psychologists have used the phrase, "giving psychology away to the public," and I've said from the beginning, "*You don't give anything to the public by standing on a street corner and just starting to talk about it. You give it away if you package it right: you give it to the media and* **they** *will dress it up—hopefully without making too many mistakes with it—and* **they** *will give it out to the general public."* The question is, how do we educate the media to recognize what are good and what are bad ideas?

While we are talking about media, I want to tell you about the new, upcoming film about the Stanford Prison Study, a docudrama called *The Stanford Prison Experiment.*

They have an excellent cast, great script, and a wonderful, new, young director named Kyle Patrick Alvarez. The team came to Stanford and we spent an entire day together. They recreated the Stanford prison yard in every exact detail. When I looked at their video, I couldn't tell it wasn't the real thing. Billy Crudup plays me, while Olivia Thirlby plays Chris.

HB: Does he do you justice? Does he capture the emotional torment that you went through?

PZ: Yes, definitely. He's really fantastic. I watched a few days of his filming.

HB: Did you give him any pointers?

PZ: Not really: the only thing I mentioned was that he didn't use his hands enough.

Questions for Discussion:

1. Do you think it will be possible to successfully integrate the core message of the Heroic Imagination Project in our educational systems? If not, what do you think the core stumbling blocks will be? Might there be some countries and systems that would be more amenable to this program than others?

2. Should psychologists make a greater formal effort to work with the media about communicating their findings? If so, how exactly? Are there any potential dangers to do so that should be taken into account?

3. Is the media's lack or rigour simply an indication of a lack of broader interest in looking more deeply at complex issues? To what extent can the commercial success of a show like **Last Week Tonight with John Oliver** *be viewed as a counterexample to this position?*

X. A New Gender Gap
Where have all the boys gone?

HB: What are you most worried about now? If there were something that you could change, what would it be?

PZ: Well, I don't think enough young people have a real sense of purpose in life, a vision that they want to follow. Perhaps that's partly because there still aren't enough good jobs. They look around and they see a political system that is unresponsive to their needs and no real sense of optimism.

In the '70s we all had great ideals. We believed that we could do something to change the world. I don't feel that now. I think people are much more narcissistic, much more narrowly focused on themselves.

The other thing that I've been focusing on recently is why boys and men, in particular are failing: all too often they're living in a world of video games and pornography, alone in a room, giving up friends, giving up even talking and chatting. This is becoming addictive and more and more widespread. Gamification has a lot of positive attributes, but not when it's in excess—and I'm not even talking about violent games, which the military are using to train people to become violent warriors.

A big concern of mine is that, in many situations I find myself in, there are almost no guys. In many psychology classes, it's now often 80% women. When I was a kid, it was maybe 55% or 60% guys to 40% women. And that's true all over. Last year more women than men got every single degree—BA, PhD, MD, business, engineering, and even computer science.

The question is, *Where have all the guys gone?* That's a question I keep asking. This is true not just in America, I think, but in other places as well. That's my biggest concern. I think boys and men need mending that we're not getting.

The other thing I discovered is that a very large percentage of boys grow up fatherless from divorce, separation, fathers being psychologically absent, or physically absent because they are travelling all the time or working two jobs.

We've learned that a mother's love is unconditional: I love you because you're my child. No matter what you do, right or wrong, you can always come home. But fathers give a lot of conditions: *You have to perform; You have to show results; You can't come home with a C or a D; You can't come home having not made the team*, or, *You can come home, but there are going to be consequences.*

All kids need a mother and a father, but I think America has the highest percentage of boys growing up fatherless—it's almost 40% or 50%—and I think that this is one of the reasons we're seeing a loss of success motivation. That's what really worries me.

HB: Unfortunately, we didn't have time to talk about the psychology of time, or shyness, or many other things, but I do hope that we'll have the opportunity to do it again. I had a great time talking to you, Phil.

PZ: Thank you—me too. Wow, I can't believe we talked for three hours non-stop. I'd hate to be the editor of all of this.

Questions for Discussion:

1. Do you share Phil's concern about the decline of men in contemporary society? To what extent might the changing gender ratios in post-secondary education, say, be more attributable to female empowerment rather than an indicator of male disempowerment?

2. In what ways has technological advance negatively impacted society? How many of these ways disproportionately affect men over women?

3. In what ways has the increased awareness of LGBTQ rights impacted how society views traditional male roles in contemporary society?

Continuing the Conversation

Readers interested in a deeper perspective on Philip's thinking are encouraged to read his many books, including: *The Lucifer Effect: How Good People Turn Evil*, *Man, Interrupted: Why Young Men are Struggling and What We Can Do About It* (with Nikita Coulombe) and *Living and Loving Better with Time Perspective Therapy: Healing from the Past, Embracing the Present, Creating an Ideal Future* (with Rosemary Sword).

Ideas Roadshow Collections

Each Ideas Roadshow collection offers 5 separate expert conversations presented in an accessible and engaging format.

- *Conversations About Anthropology & Sociology*
- *Conversations About Astrophysics & Cosmology*
- *Conversations About Biology*
- *Conversations About History, Volume 1*
- *Conversations About History, Volume 2*
- *Conversations About History, Volume 3*
- *Conversations About Language & Culture*
- *Conversations About Law*
- *Conversations About Neuroscience*
- *Conversations About Philosophy, Volume 1*
- *Conversations About Philosophy, Volume 2*
- *Conversations About Physics, Volume 1*
- *Conversations About Physics, Volume 2*
- *Conversations About Politics*
- *Conversations About Psychology, Volume 1*
- *Conversations About Psychology, Volume 2*
- *Conversations About Religion*
- *Conversations About Social Psychology*
- *Conversations About The Environment*
- *Conversations About The History of Ideas*

All collections are available as both eBook and paperback.

www.ingramcontent.com/pod-product-compliance
Lightning Source LLC
Chambersburg PA
CBHW020246030426
42336CB00010B/643